Additional Praise for *Portals*

I have seen Sean Sexton's ranch and witnessed what he calls "my sheltering in the broad arms of family and land." Call him a cowboy poet if you will: the ethos and narrative of a place he knows and loves distill in him and pass through the lens of his specific and gentle light. Mornings speak, as do laboring heifers, swallows, and grass itself. Whitman of the Florida prairie, Jimenez of the hammock, Sexton makes of a common experience a monument. His poems are potent, enspirited, unflinching, necessarily elegiac, encompassing. This is a beautiful collection I will treasure.

—Janisse Ray, author of *A House of Branches* & *Red Lanterns*

A true cowman, the depth of Sean Sexton's experienced eye offers rare details to the rich reward of a rancher's life—heretofore overlooked in the arena of cowboy poetry. Offering joy and humor, the basic facts of caring for cattle are often interspersed with his broad range of musings and a sense of satisfaction and connection to art and literature from the outside world. These poems become a diverse journey across a natural landscape and way of life. I am so pleased and proud his voice speaks so well of our cattle culture and demonstrates the subsequent solace acquired by a disappearing breed of men and women with his well-hewn, hands-on poetry.

—John Dofflemyer, Dry Crik Press

sean sexton

p o r t a l s

poems

For Eric   3/10/23

*with admiration of your
fine work and
best regards
for Florida's Future*

— Sean

Press 53
—◦—
Winston-Salem

Press 53, LLC
PO Box 30314
Winston-Salem, NC 27130

First Edition

Cover image, "Decoration II," by author, 2018

Author Photo by Bob Stone

Library of Congress Control Number
2022951304

Printed on acid-free paper
ISBN 978-1-950413-57-7

For Sharon—always,

and
Georgia Marie, Olivia Evelyn,
and Emerson Tate

Acknowledgments

The author thanks the editors of the publications where these poems first appeared, occasionally in different form:

Chariot Press, "And Now Our Aged House"

Cimarron Review, "Yesterday Morning"

Florida Review, "Pictures of the Early Gods of Our Adolescence"

Kestrel, "Holes" & "This Land"

Lightning Key Review, "Color of the World Sestina"

Of Poets & Poetry, "Voices"

Panoply, "Eating the Heifer"

Ran Off With the Star Bassoon, "Capital Gain"

South Florida Poetry Journal, "RFK/RIP"

Susurrus, "Plea," "Pine Heart," "Verities" & "Remains of Barney"

The Blue Mountain Review, "Sonnet on a Glass Snake [with a Line from Derek Walcott]"

The Night Heron Barks, "Semen Testing the Herd Bulls," "Fools Day" & "Old Cow Museum"

The Nature Readings Project/AVIEWFROMTHISWILDERNESS.COM, "Black on Black, White on White" & "Branding"

The Stratford Quarterly, "Departure"

Vita Poetica, "Ars Poetica, Obstetrics, Painting and the Rough Draft" & "Libélula"

Vox Populi, "Poem Letter to Rick Campbell" & "Hillside Equipment Auction outside Dothan, Alabama"

Additional and grateful acknowledgment to those involved in musical productions and performances featuring the author's original poetry:

"Dirge," was set to music and performed by singer-songwriter Frank Hogans, Baltimore, MD.

"Bright Future" was featured in *Chasing Light: Poems inspired by Burgert Brothers photographs*, Yellow Jacket Press, edited by Gianna Russo.

"Branding," "Fence," "Noise," and "Canoe Creek Road" were featured in *Cowboy Solstice,* a livestream poetry and music concert presented in the 2020 Summer Concert Series, Community Church, Vero Beach, FL.

"Voices" was filmed and recorded to inaugurate the Laura Riding Jackson Foundation *Featured Poets* series presenting past poets of the annual Laura Riding Jackson Foundation Poetry and Barbeque. The series was created in response to COVID-19 and cancellation of the 2020 10th annual Poetry and Barbeque event. Lauraridingjackson.org

"Dilemma," "Firing the Hay Spots," and "Branding" were featured in a June 6, 2021, recorded session of *Great American Folk Show*, Medora, North Dakota.

"Capital Gain" was featured in a November 2021 recorded session featuring a conversation with North Dakota poet Shadd Piehl, for the *Great American Folk Show*, Medora, North Dakota.

"Voices" and "Yesterday Morning" were featured in a streamed program for young writers as a nature-journaling collaborative between the Laura Riding Jackson Foundation and Pelican Island Audubon Society.

"Yesterday Morning," Firing the Hay Spots," "Cleaning Out from beneath the Scales," "Shit," "Black on Black, White on White," "Naming," "Eating the Heifer," "In Yonder Fields," and "This Land" were featured in a live-streamed program entitled "Beautiful Morning," taped November 12, 2020, for the 37th National Cowboy Poetry Gathering before a live audience in the sanctuary of the Community Church, Vero Beach, FL.

"Eating the Heifer" and "All Things Are Found in All Things" were featured in *Decade: Ten Years of Poetry and Barbeque*, The Seizin Press Vero, Laura Riding Jackson Foundation.

"Bright Future," "Pictures of the Early Gods of Our Adolescence," and "Branding" received 2020 Pushcart Prize nominations.

"Eating the Heifer," "Sonnet on a Glass Snake," and "RFK/RIP" received 2021 Pushcart Prize nominations.

"How Strange We Live So Long to Know" was set to choral music written and arranged by composer Rick Sowash, Cincinnati, Ohio.

"Sonnet on a Glass Snake," "The Mast," and "Hillside Equipment Auction Yard outside Dothan, Alabama" were featured in *America's Song*, "The South," performed and recorded November 12, 2021, Community Church, Vero Beach, FL.

Special thanks to my many friends in poetry, always willing to listen to or read my next poem. I haven't room to list you all. Warren Obluck, Alice Friman, Alfred Corn, Rick Campbell, Cathy Smith Bowers, Claude Wilkinson, Shadd Piehl, Steve Bradbury, Sidney Wade, Andy Wilkinson, Brian Turner, Cherie CIark, Susan Boyd, Laurel Blossom, and Janisse Ray I must name here. Christopher Forrest, my editor, and Kevin Morgan Watson at Press 53, I adore you.

Contents

Departure

The Wedding Dance

Portals

Coda

A child said, What is the grass? fetching it to me with full hands;
How could I answer the child? I do not know what it is any more than he.
. . . .
And now it seems to me the beautiful uncut hair of graves.

—Walt Whitman, "Song of Myself"

Naming

Chosen Aubade

Yesterday I stepped out a moment and saw the moon
at whichever end of the yard, I've forgotten,
and whether morning or night,
the same ashen light.

I say dawn; the thin orange fingernail—trimmed
from its digit—just over the field
thumbing down the gloom,
if I am right.

Semen Testing the Herd Bulls

Everything that matters in life flows through tubes.
—Georg Lichtenberg

We get an early start.
Each, driven from seclusion,
congenial as flood-staged rivers,
they set in motion on lumbering trajectories
to the gate. We push them in trios and quartets—
bellowing down the lane—a rider betwixt
to stage them strategically in the pens. Once
arrived, the usual upstart gets thrown through a fence.

And they fill the hopper one by one, brought up
the runway, a bull at a time for the test, as others
wait like the elderly on their scripts at the chemist.
Some barely fit the squeeze, poled behind, palpated
before insertion of the probe, then three moments,
three rocking pulses, a crystalline slide of half-lives
in the lens. *I see a whole semi-load of calves!*
is the shout. Boss says, *Worm him and turn him out.*

Naming

Old Boss bought twenty-five open heifers
from Gilbert Tucker and a month later
won his bid for the two best bulls
at the University sale in Gainesville.
He was suddenly in the purebred Brahma
business. The day came to brand, name,
and register the first crop of calves and he
brought a baby book to the pens for ideas,
ignoring convention to descend renowned
old titles and strains of the breed: *Manso,*
Imperator, Loxacrata, and *Reloto,*
Wrinkles, Burma Ben, and *Little Bozo.*

Bull calves became heroes from the Bible
mythology and silver screen: *Hector, Hercules,*
Sampson, and *Rambo.* He called
a late-born, ill-natured, reddish-tinted bull
Aldrich, and we queried, *Why that?*
He replied, *There was this feller at the Phi-Delt*
house when I was going to school
who looked and acted just like him,
and Aldrich was his name.

On the other end of the pedigree, he named
heifer calves after favorite girlfriends:
Carol Ann, Nancy, Betty, Hazel, and *Vernice.*
The Countess was a childhood flame
down on her luck, descended from royalty,
stranded in Florida with only a story.
Another became *Delta Dawn,* for the tune
he'd sing any hour of the day: *She's forty-one*
and her daddy still calls her baby.

Color of the World Sestina

Blood is inside the world flowing,
waking and brightening the dark.
And rain sharpens the grass, hiding
drought, stealing color, filling
barren fields; to clothe them in plenty.
What is most alive, which the dying?

What is the color of the world? Death
is sumptuous and grand, yellow flows
from entrails of a crushed moth, plenty
escaping, like water from ice. Darkness
is swollen with shadow—full
in surrounding light—yet hidden.

But dark and light never hide
from bright, insistent death.
Napoleon was color-blind, saw full
fields of blood like grass, flowing,
greening a garden of killing—darkened
with harm, ruin aplenty.

Blue is the night in day, the plenteous,
eye of heaven, olden, hiding
in the unseeable dark.
And morning is but light dying
into night, where all color flows
like fallen rain—filling

ground high and low—as grass fills
fields, seeds drop, vanish into plenty
to emerge and rise shimmering, flowing
toward winter and ice, hidden
again in fading light; lost to death,
dwindling in darkness.

Color buries in light, darkens,
wanes, vanishes in fulsome
night where ice has grown to die
in the bright. But light, plentiful,
changes, falls, fails, hiding
like blood inside, ever flowing,

closed in dark, dead only to rise and fill
the morning, hide the night, flow from
plenty into color of the world.

Black on Black, White on White

They emerge from the womb's prism
into shining light—
yea black by black,
red of red, white from white,
and strike the ground like lightning,
in dazzling color: cream spilt in the grass,
beige, terra cotta, coffee and coal. Heaven's
fawning kiss, deepest, darkest twilit pelts,
strewn with stars, phases-of-the-moon-setting
foreheads, sorrel horizons, brockle-faced,
pieded and bald, two-toned, watermarked,
whole legs of alabaster, pizzles dipped in ivory,
deckle-edges, roan underlines, lace and finery.
Bovine conventions in every hue, done
in mauve, pink, saffron, and circles round the sun.

Have you never seen a purple cow?

All the while as
we put black with black,
white on white, red to red
thinking to have our way
in this world—
we were breeding rainbows.

Verities

It has to be beautiful.
—Wendell Berry

Running the fence through early mist
ahead of the herd to open a gate,
I pass a glittering, dew-kissed
web, other prisms hung, each—
in any likely reach, loveliness
with no constraint.

Yet in a moment-turned thought,
I see humble tenancy,
a fisherman's tattered net, just-
mended and set, or vendor's
rude stands—only their hands
—astir in the wakening city.

———

And the shining band of ibises
appearing suddenly
in front of the rooming house
lawn—had a summons been issued
on a standing army to fill languid
mornings with beauty?

They advance in formation
brandishing rosy weaponry
probing the greensward in unison.
And with no time for applause,
they've flown from our eyes,
off to the grand emergency.

The Sheep Business in Florida

We bought Tom Forester's sheep when he passed;
his widow priced them under duress.
Bred for the tropics—a small, mongrel strain—
raised on weeds, wild bananas, and maiden cane,
in a fallow tract of citrus
at the edge of town to the west.

We hauled them to a pasture by the house
the yard dog soon into them, cost us
a lamb to realize to run them with cattle,
and stow safe between horn and tail.
Workdays we brought them all to the pens,
and turned in with the calves when we parted them.

We wormed, bobbed lambs' tails, castrated the rams,
and soon relished dinners of mutton and lamb.
For shearing we fashioned a rude wooden bench
to bind the ewe's legs whenever they'd flinch,
and ran the clippers, dabbing nicks with grease
during slow, meager accruals of fleece.

Day's end sent fifty ewes up the lane—
wounded, despoiled, clothed only in shame
—toward lessening days and cooler weather
to flesh their brood and mend their coiffure.
The measly reap, after many weeks,
sent by Greyhound bus in old muslin sacks,

bound to a factory in the far north,
forty-five cents a pound, FOB, all its worth.
Slaughter mornings in the crowding pen shade,
I held throats and Uncle Eddie the blade.
One afternoon, like a razor along a fence,
a lightning strike put us half out of business.

Strewing its length with burnt bones and wool
of thirty-five sheep and our best herd bull.
Old boss reckoned to improve his lot,
fitted the ranch truck with a handmade crate,
and we drove the eastern seaboard lands
to fetch a three hundred-pound Shenandoah ram.

The first week in service, he suddenly died,
soon the whole harem began dropping like flies.
In six months' time two wethers remained
secreting in the dark, out grazing by day.
We left them alone to do as they would,
and quit the sheep business in Florida for good.

Prodigal

We called him *Bill Clinton* after
he left his drove
for the neighbor's
cows down the road;

broke every fence—with no regard
of consequence—
to ply his trade
and cast his seed.

But was found unimpeachable
the coming year,
He'd bred every
cow, far and near.

Monday

A soft tone from the bedstead wakens me and I scroll
through messages—nothing important—no cows out
on the road—no one calling me. As I'm pulling on
my socks—puzzled from the fusty pile on the floor—
it lights again. I scroll to *Important notice—malicious
spyware*, it says. A candidate pleads, *I am humbly asking . . .*
before a sudden jingle with a drop-down weather report—
Light rain to begin 5:35 a.m.

I turn off the phone, step out the door into moist air
sifting through the trees. A single truck passes along
the distant road headed to the mine to wait in the dark.
The sky seems to be lightening every glance east. Moments
pass, little windows begin to open in the haze over
the pasture across the way as if a large apartment building
could be standing there beside the edge of a hidden city,
but it's only the morning.

Soon we'll decamp to the fields, survey weekend arrivals
of calves: infancies of wet, untagged ears on shaky little
heads. And we'll record into a book we carry: the news,
how welcome that noun escapes its bitter plurality
of words grown from the ether as these creatures appear
without notification to find, apprehend, and register to
another human end, and the reigning march of hours spread
into light upon a gathering wind.

Letter to Rick Campbell

This little chore, picking through your poems as you asked, gave
me something to do in my almost nightly 2 AM insomnia.
Curse the importune wakenings of late middle age! Or is it early old age?
Thus, I've read again in this ungainly hour your words and life,
seeing the amazing journey it has been as I ponder my own,
my sheltering in the broad arms of family and land.

I had to kill a cow yesterday, or I should say, I watched my son
shoot her after we were unable to get her on her feet.
Bulls rode her down when by that unfortunate clock—
suckling her twelfth calf in her fourteenth year—she came in heat.
We hauled water and feed to her three days, administered
Banamine, Dexamethasone injectable, roll-on gel, and a whole
caulking gun of calcium paste, and with tractor and forks tried to lift
her to her feet with a cruel cradling device borrowed from a dairy.
We failed.

But I'm off subject now and I want to tell you to come and read us
these vital, riveting poems I've chosen from your books
for a program at church. They speak of burning rivers, molten steel,
revelations in a city window, a lost brother, magnolias and loblolly
pines, your beloved daughter, and measures of time. They mark worlds
uncharted where I'm from, doors left open—to one caught behind gates
that must be kept shut, and visions of a grand, boundless sphere, to one
who's memorized the dawn and set of day from one lifelong horizon.

The passages contained in these lines—I now see as your own little
circumscribing strings of fence—astound me; enlighten as they
sadden, hurt as they gladden. A soft-spoken vision runs their gamut
to the end of your pages yet, by your gifts, stays within reach, as the ruckus
of the interstate in the distance when the wind is out of the west
on such a morning as this.

Fool's Day

Was it they'd mostly finished their work, how
the bulls came along this morning, let themselves
be driven back to their pasture still in ruin with
holes dug from last year's nine-month layoff?
It finishes for some the way it began, chasing an
elderly dam in heat through one gate and out another,
but not today in this last feral wind of the season.

Now we see them making their places out there
as we add the heifer bulls, out of scale with their mentors,
threadbare from hard winter pursuit. There will be
posturing, momentary jousts, but they seem to know it's
over, the heat of day soon to replace this half-feigned
détente and settle them into a morbid peace cast
upon everything present.

This Land

Having no literary past to speak of, no
ruin or olden scroll buried in this land
find the imprint of fallen leaves, news
shining in the grass; rumors cast
amid shimmering fronds.

With no forespoken hardness, no igneous
heavenward reaches and bereft of precious
mineral and ore, look to swollen clouds
in the distance, or glassine, horizonless
underlands, empty as a widow's joy.

Heed *here today, gone tomorrow* whispers
in the air, fading voices in a shoaling river,
overtaken metes and bounds where tree-
telling ditches and nothing less recent amble
through headland and marsh to a murmuring sea.

Nothing happened here that isn't happening now.

Forsake all allusion and memory, doubt
any worth of this land, save the fervent mist,
half-hiding, half-revealing abandoned dreams
now consigned to the sky. Wonder anew if this day
or another begins your journey to a directionless
realm, a final embarkation into light.

Shall we fall from the world like a stone, fail time
as a weakening heart and be lost, one place to another?
Is life but a lapse upon a crust, set beside a dark
selvage where we've been ever flowing, *water-like*
to the end of the eye, gathering mindward
as we go, a barely-remembered story.

English isn't

         God's first language.
Perhaps not the linguist we'd imagine,
but *Gardener* as Dobyns said, most
nouns given to foliage, throaty vowels
of the golden mean, mineral consonants
issuing to the wind, speaking always
for themselves, but greatest of all: silence—
the original tongue crying everywhere,
         everything, never heard.

for Naomi

Fired Words

Young Angry Bull

Then the beast shall arise

take a determined angle

upon all our device—

tear something all to hell

—and we come to see how little

we comprehend the universe.

Firing the Hay Spots

On the day of the feast of the annunciation

Undoing a measure of waste—
made in winter's dire,
as we ill-afford a burnt place
upon the pasture's pale green face,
and set remains afire.

Whereupon all season
cows gathered in hay-parties,
cavorting in unison
ruining bales like young
planets seized on delivery.

Ripping the air with
their dry-grass coughs,
fodder and manure,
and hard-trodden water
fattened into sloughs.

Roll upon roll, set
on the andirons of dirt, after
Ash Wednesday and Lent,
and drought came and went.
They disappeared like laughter.

Now we send a flame walking
across cobbled ground
to free the battened covering—
waken vernal drowsing
and let new again be found.

Sound

And then a *crack*
rends the day: sudden,
mortal, undoing a morning's
work, setting in motion
a week, month, lifetime
of ruin.

New sound.
Strange,
beyond hearing,
beyond tiny bones
beating in the ear.
A felling,

spouse's moan,
mother's sob. Sound
of the end of sound.
Something seen
breaking loose
from the heart.

Branding

for Carol Frost

Each touch of the iron to clarify,
yet too much and the mark smears,
slurs permanently
upon the years,

so one winter morning, birthling
just caught and tagged at her feet
and you can't know what, long
ago on her hip, you meant to speak.

Flinching interminable
through skin-thin pain,
of the black cattle
as you apply again and again,

but brahmas take fire like a pine,
still as a summer morning:
all that elegance a moon,
held fast and shining

in the cage. Each number taken
like medicine, our palaver
to be seen every
moment thereafter.

Some come *baby-haired,* numbers
hidden like birds in a thicket
revealed with flame, sulfurous
smoke, the autonomic kick

slamming the back of the chute
with each burn. So brutal:
you on the other end of that
would waken in the hospital.

First printings lightly given
to tell where numerals sit:
up, down, side by side, often
miswritten with mishandled heat.

Others: crisp, tan-leathered
figures perfectly placed:
furnaced, ordered,
clearly said,

so you think:
that seems beautiful to me
and think again:
can such a thing be?

Pine Heart

Those hard remains from a former
state of the world—
years concentrated, scattered
over boundless tracts, where

they say, a squirrel could run
branch to branch, gulf to ocean
through stands of ancient pine,
relics the cold brings to mind,

unearthed, or gathered like eggs
when chill breaks upon the days
and the light rises
recalling the true universe:

all warmth fugitive, fleeting.
Yet that sweetened air
returns to neighborhood evenings
in smoky malinger.

Now the fallen tree, driven around
two summers since the wind,
cut and stacked with rotted-
off posts, the pile revisited.

Quickly a wood-yard, made in a clearing,
and that confection again, opening
from split chunks of pine
flayed and strewn like something slain.

By sharpened iron, angle, and swing
to divine the grain; all our wanting
illusory. One only need find a door—
between each knot—great things in store.

Fired Words

for Shadd Piehl

King James burns
much slower than
the Revised
Standard Version.

Shakespeare, and Dante
by canto and play
could warm you through
a good winter's day,

or the whole O. E. D.,
A to Z, with
annotations and appendices,
a regular North Dakota blizzard.

Ordeal

Heaven ordained it, and we fought it:
The heifer I found in the last minute of a
Friday afternoon before my plan to leave town,
her uterus prolapsed, massive, blood-blackened
cotyledons, all hanging to her ankles, a full
day's struggle in her demeanor. My son was
on his honeymoon and no one else on hand,
so I called Emory Bailes:
It will take a while, he said, *we're just finishing
a fence, but I will come before dark and bring
plenty of help.*

We got a rope on her and she came to life,
tore from our hands, her insides out, leaping
at every bound. By the sight, CL declared: *She's
a dead cow!* I thought we'd quit right then, but he added
When we get her caught—we'll try to put it back.
We pulled her down, and the crew piled on, settled
into the task, slipped a clean feed sack beneath, doused
the mass with iodine wash, and sugared—three grocery
store cartons worth—all that anger in white
crystals so it seemed a giant raspberry Danish
slowly seeping fluid, shrinking imperceptibly.

She struggled, as two men held her down, straddling
like survivors on a swamped dory in a sea of grass.
Three of us behind, working in unison—folding
the thing together, as one kept pushing it back in,
keeping careful fingers so as not to tear through
the tissue and kill her—all of it twice as hard as pulling
something free. We took shifts, fighting our exhaustion
but made little headway—every gain, spilled back
with each retracted arm, every hope and wish drowned
in the undertow.

Emory found a birthling wandering in the grass, bleating
like a lost lamb, caught him in two throws and brought
him over to us. He kneeled to strip colostrum out of her,
while we worked, milking her into a soda bottle
switching teats to keep the flow until tired, sticky
fingers gave out, but he'd drawn a portion and the calf
took it like a starved pup.

I told him, *He's yours if you want him.*
He said, *I got two others I'm raising I can put him with.*

In the end, we didn't save her—we barely helped ourselves.
She just died, one of the boys up front said.
You sure?
Yeah—she's gone.
We stopped pushing and all stood up. She gave a sigh
in soft reflex, legs then thrashing space and someone said,
If we leave her like this, she won't quit till tomorrow morning.
We ain't got a gun among us, said another.
CL had a sharp knife, and at my beckon,
I watched a second throat get cut in as many days.
It had been a decade since the last.

Eating the Heifer

—heart, tongue, tripe,
the brown liver and kidneys, grown
and picked from her dark garden like varieties
of fruit. Striped, pebbled, and squared stacks
of knuckle, rib, and tail come shrink-wrapped
and quick-frozen by the abattoir as if they
devised her into large pieces of candy
and unblinking eyes of bone set
in penumbras of flesh, sectioned
like saw logs with guardian haloes of fat—
seemly atmospheres of a fresh-sliced planet.
There is all her fear in our teeth, toughness
they couldn't kill sent home in six coolers.

Her inbred anxiety shot through at the end
redeemed for chewing, and how she balked
at every gate we set for her like malicious
gods. Only the liver, marrow, and sweet-
breads and the autonomic heart remain pliant,
sovereign from harm, tender as forgiveness.
We take her in, savoring every part—bisques,
roasts, tartare, jerks and grinds; sop her juices
like spring melt from mountainside seeps,
soaking attendant carrots, spuds and onions
as easily, she joins back to the roots of creation
becomes nourishment and medicine—our
peace and succor.

Midwife made of meat, she births us backward
through hunger, her last poem spoken every
swallow as she increases and grows in us, very
things we devour—chine and cartilage, blood
and cell. There is no greater magic in the world
than this: to chew of her the forbs, legumes,
and delicacies her mother taught her in the bright
morning, the shade-sweetened lea. Masticate
the light, imbibe the rain, smell the evening mist
rising from the caldron as she steams and softens
in the kitchen air. Listen to her singing
to the fire from the grate, arias of the earth's
original music borne of this world, making
again into something new.

Haplessness

*That boy can't pick up a damn thing ain't got a
handle on it.*
                    —Gene Golnick

They become sudden second-class citizens,
who walk through the front gate of the pens,
leave it open . . .

Old Boss's remedy, so vicious and swift
you'd need only one treatment for
a permanent fix.

And those who head straight toward and into a *stuckey*
as if there was nothing to know of the ground.
Fatherless perhaps. Flunky

of what should come natural; *cain't hook a chain around a log,*
drive a nail straight, or have the good sense
to be quiet around the livestock,

lacking in what can't be told or learned. Orphaned
from ways of the world yet about to find them out—
missing the turn, falling in holes, ever headed

like a sick calf to a ditch. Nestling of the hard way down,
flesh at road's edge, adder that crawled
too late or too soon.

O hapless ones—ever lost, never where supposed,
how do we love you and bring
you close?

The heart is a tricky place to start, with hands
all too ready to cut
you loose.

Untitled Poem

for Naomi Shihab Nye

Life is brutal.

Because hornets sting—the little *fighter-jet* kind
with nasty tempers that build summer fortresses
in metal gates and under eaves of mineral sheds,

where beasts are in danger for a lick of salt, *Air Force
overhead* ever-ready to strike, and men risk leaning
in to dispense more from sacks when supplies run low,

one must bring a pole to push out nests full
of larvae, half made wasp-children growing
in the cells.

We commit them to the mercy of the ants—
which is no mercy at all—as *felling the house
tames the bite.*

And everything keeps to its way: wasps hard-wired to their fate,
we with our jobs to do, and ruined tabernacles bristling with
creation—lost to the world—so we say:

Life is brutal.

Voices

Hidden

We make our Monday rounds to rope, tag, and record
the weekend arrival of calves, invade a cagey young heifer's
solitude, her swollen udder and mucus string amid smears
of umbilicus confirm an air of deceit. *She's hollow*, my son
says, same as his grandpa would say a lifetime ago.

Now the game is on:
something she's hiding in her face as she feints away toward some
vague apparition on the horizon.
You's a lie! Uncle Eddie would call out to her little ruse when
they were his days, his calves to find.

We search shaded hollows in the coffee weeds, check among
smut grass clumps, late-summer deeps filling the pasture like
a moon-driven tide. He could be anywhere, everywhere and
sometimes we must abandon our quest out of fear of finding
by running him over.

With one eye, she's watching—comes running when our mock
bleating draws her out. We believe we're getting close, as she's
suddenly more animate, then fades. *Warm or cold?* we wonder,
hunting like a lion to get the drop on things of a world both
generous and stingy—

only a different day might bring a mortal chase—should he find
some infant thing in its hiding place.
No less a grazer rushing the opened gate ahead of the throng to a fresh
ditch-bottom where sweetened lengths await, or crow searching to steal
what the mockingbird spent all season to conceal.

Herman Thomas Weighs In

He arrives on market day,
stops to open the rear gate
of his truck, backs to the loading chute—
gets out and says:

*I'm working for the government
and the insurance company.*

*Sean—There are more educated fools
than fools educated.
If you ain't gonna do shit today
get up and get an early start.*

Thinking of Summer at the Beginning of Winter

for Charles Wright

I've waited all season for this cool, I told Deon Vickers
when he came to buy bulls.
Yeah, but now the grass has quit growing!

We stand on the brink of ruin, light and warmth
vanished together. Cries sound the distance.
Drought has become the cold's accomplice.

Tomorrow is a fearful thing; summer was
but an extended outing in another land, where
we were only visitors knowing we'd have to leave.

We cannot open a gate to anywhere but here,
and watch them pass through as if they were
going somewhere, yet not a head down to graze.

February looms like a mountain range in the distance; March
imponderable in this scathing wind and indolent spring.
We're in the spite of time.

Canoe Creek Road

This is poetry's weather, this its true home . . .
                    —Derek Walcott

Where the town breaks off, and the road turns north, the prairie
commences. Rusted, dagger-sharp cadmium yellow florets
arm the palmetto expanses in this parched condition. Tawny
and drab notes of myrtle and broom sedge
key a sparse, unheard music upon that acuity.
Soft, newly made green adorns islands of cypress
moored in the distance like earthbound clouds,
fashioned as if from slumber by scarcity's embrace.

Have I driven to this drought with a solution in tow empurpling the east?
North, from Locusee, a morning thunder burst
extending the dark ten miles to the intersection.
By all appearances, more rain is on the way. The plain stretches
along, belying its secret possession of three lakes: Marian,
Jackson, and Kissimmee out beyond sight, chained together
with creeks and sloughs, passages through the underworld
to lost realms of the Calusa, threading cypress and bayhead.

Each mile brings signal changes in terrain, pine stands, upbraiding
space, and, as if a lunatic had run amok with paint out there, broad
white bands set at eye-level mark every twentieth tree in assay
of red-cockaded woodpecker nests; other indices of extremity.
There's evidence of a burn, the cut just inside the fence:
a sugar sand gouge breaking east, circumscribing acres
of scorched ground driven under influence of fire to the horizon;
already the world's prodigies begin to return, greening

cabbage tree buds, needles, and sproutlings of grass save where
flames grew fierce, climbed like monkeys through the candelabra.
Trees cluster in ruined intervals standing upon quiet repair:
The foolishness of heaven is greater than the wisdom of man.
Up ahead, as if the blackened ground had spawned its animus,
a coven of vultures scrimmage upon last night's roadside casualty.
A next mile of small bridges straddling creek crossings bring levity
of umber pools amassing pond flags, lilies, and violet blooms set amid
bright flashing of pickerel weed. A giant lizard drowses at water's edge.

———

Remembrances of Kenansville's centennial last fall:
We arrived at the stretch of road near the tail end of a parade
along *Flagler Avenue*, once the main street of *Whittier*, Osceola
County's first settlement. Half the citizenry was in mounted
procession, the other half watching. Grand Marshalls Russell
Clayton, Thelma Harvey, and Louise Sever passed in a convertible,
waving. Brighten Mick, Little Miss Silver Spurs; Karlie Heaberlin,
Miss Congeniality; and First Runner-up, Mackenzie Garmany, carried
flags of Florida, the nation, and Silver Spurs Rodeo, in full regalia.

The celebration filled the yard of the schoolhouse Mary Lily Kenan,
Henry Flagler's wife, gave six thousand dollars to build. Settlers renamed
the town *Kenansville* in 1914 in her honor. We saw Billy Davis selling
his spurs, Iris Wall telling stories, Paul Vickers in a *flowerdy* shirt sitting
his cracker horse, and the grandnephew of Lawrence Silas, a famous
cattleman born of slaves, in attendance. Old-timers held court as a
menu of beans, pulled pork, swamp cabbage, and guava cobbler fed
five hundred under a huge tent. A time capsule with pictures and
mementos from all the town's folk—to be opened in twenty-five
years, was buried in the lawn out front.

Gentrification begins farther north as mailboxes appear, first
solitary and few, then formal entrances of lintel and post
aggrandizing names of old families: Partin, Bass, Harvey,
Overstreet, Bronson and Whaley. Shell roads on rutted trajectories
cross cleared ground diving deep into woods toward homesteads
hidden beyond outlying barns and pens. Implements, live or dead
in their tracks and elevated tanks of fuel or syrup mitigate a plenary
emptiness save for the distant, blinking, omniscient, cell tower.

Briar-covered heaps of palmettos, and stumps, from long-ago cleared
rights of way punctate a mile-long line of open ground, just heeled-
in grass cultivars from some horticultural Orient, bet on bottomless
tracts of silica and scrub where *all you can raise is the price.*
Soon the road and the *Sunshine State Parkway* interlace
twisting over and under like lengthy strands of a plaited whip,
separations drawn close by the same drainages, swamps and stands,
each arteriole, another blood course of a thirsty land.

Billboards peek through the outback in occasional glimpses messaging
dichotomies of dog-bite lawyers, rescue of the unborn, and half-priced
tickets to the *worlds*, set on the soft, momentary, geology of the
peninsula, places where human aspiration, industry, and hope pass
through on a southerly, two-hundred-mile declension into expanses
of sawgrass and drowning islands set beside a burgeoning metropolis.
Every platted acre and grab of ground uncover slender history set
upon the next thousand second-comings of the sea.

———

The road presses on past cow pens, turf farms, a sand quarry,
and turnoffs to public boat ramps on distant lakes. Day workers
with goosenecks trailers full of horses and gear and semi-rigs with
pallets of sod fly by in the oncoming lane. A large compound of layer
houses stands empty behind double gates, locked on a failed egg-
economy, near the Melbourne-to-Orlando high-tension line;
a transfer station within a fenced gravel yard close by. The creek
runs through locks, along rubble banks on an ambling course from
Lake Cypress to Lake Gentry. In unnatural undoing of land and time,

civilization happens all at once. Ranchettes, mini-mansions: *One man's
dream, another man's nightmare.* Realty signs increase as native tracts
succumb to whole walled and gated communities. Intersections turn
into hubs of second-growth business—feed supply store becomes gas
depot, hardware store turns mini-mart. Amenities accrue closer to town:
schools, churches, shopping plazas, and a new fire station. The road
widens on approach to St. Cloud, "The soldier friendly city," with new
traffic signals and turn lanes at every intersection.

In 1887, the town, namesake of St. Cloud, Minnesota, was founded
by Hamilton Disston. He built a sugar plantation and railroad to carry
cane to market. The '93 Panic and '94-95 Freeze demised the industry
and in 1909, thirty-five thousand acres, bought by the *Seminole Land
and Investment Company* became site for the *Grand Army of the
Republic Veteran's Colony,* selected for *Health, Climate, and
Productiveness of Soil.* Streets were named for state's soldiers served,
and Canoe Creek Road became Vermont Avenue four blocks from
Highway 192 in the center of town.

———

Headed home from the Beef Council meeting in Kissimmee, I retrace
footsteps through light and heat, furnaced in the late western orb.
Holopaw, Illeyaw, Nittaw, Yee Haw, and *Ossawa*—mythic Indian
settlements passed on the way to and beyond the Desert Inn at the
Crossroads where once, Bill Keene, just a child in a crew driving
cattle from Grape Hammock to Ft. Pierce, stopped for the night:
*We slept out under the stars and took off early that morning
taking the herd south on the 441 grade. At midday, three of us
rode up alongside a truck threading through the herd and loaded
with watermelons—we handed off four. The driver never knew!*

Bill just bought a bull and made us wait to load him until he told
his story. He said they *stopped at noon and ate watermelons for
dinner in the shade.*

Capital Gain

Old Boss said: "I went into Elmer Bowers office. He was the only accountant in town at the time—the old kind with a green eyeshade and garters on his sleeves. I said, 'Elmer I want to set up a Capital Gains bookkeeping system for my cowherd.' He replied, 'OK Ralph. If you want to do that, you're going to have to number every cow and write them down in a record book and when you buy a cow, you're going to have to list what you paid for her in the book, and when you sell one, you're going to have put down what you got.' So I went home and it took Uncle Eddie and me two weeks, working with a running iron—we didn't have number irons back then. We laid a lightered-knot fire and penned and branded every cow. I set up a ledger and wrote down all the numbers. At the end of the year, I went to town, and carried that book with me, walked into Elmer's office, handed it to him and said, 'Here, I've done it.' He opened it, scanned a few pages and said, 'Well I'll be Goddamned!'"

Cleaning Out from beneath the Scales

We won't condemn them, but they're weighing 30 pounds light—
figured you'd want to get them fixed.
                              —Ryan DeSutter, FDA Scales Inspector

This morning we slide the ancient floor-
planks off the metal frame to open to
the insipid, breathless surface below;
the foundation and rails under
the gate corner buried in dirt.
I dig between buckled ancient
backbone sills rousing ant lions
and tiny, colorless toads, hand ten
five-gallon bucketsful to my son
to fill hollows in the outer lane.
Together we move what amassed
in a year, carried in mud and dust.

The scale-bearings are frozen in a she-
rodent's nest work: dry sticks, grass stems,
leaves and a large blue chunk of Styrofoam,
jammed in the theory of the thing. I reach
from my knees and clear them with three
ritual tools from the weigh-box: a mason's
spatula, long, thin screwdriver, and wooden
handled, swallow-forked trowel, cached
to poke and clean crevices, scrape surfaces
and grade the excess into low places
beneath the joists where it can do no harm.
The work is hot and humid. I emerge
like a chimney sweep, covered in grime.

A folded correction notice left
by the man from the Department
of Weights and Measures states,
Livestock Scale/Fairbanks Morse.
Serial# 1341E Model 116532
Tolerance—*Maintenance*
Device Accuracy Violation—*Fail/*
Device Status—*Rejected Performance*
Comments: *Please trim back trees*
and bushes on left side of scale
before notifying for reinspection.
They limit access for the crane
and weights. Signed,

Ryan DeSutter / Inspector

———

One year we had to incarcerate
Split Ear in the scale house, only place
on the ranch he couldn't escape
after he caught an urge three weeks
ahead of breeding season, got with cows
one morning and set about his business.
We drove him to the bull pasture,
but he was back the next day. Four
trips to jail wouldn't dry him out
each stay worsening his cell—water
and feed fouled, walls plastered
with frenzied manure. His bellowing
rang through the barnyard until we gave in
put out the bulls a week early.
The next year, forty calves out of season
accounted for his pain and prodigy.

The scales remain askew after all our work.
We unhook the column of cast-iron counter-
weights, discover the bottom set hollow
with a removable lid—spill its ballast
of ephemera—filled sixty-five years ago
with split-shot sinkers, fish-hooks, nails, tacks,
screws, bearing balls, chunks of a shattered magnet
and nibs of lead. We add to its contents, yet
reassembled and hung—the arm plummets.

Margins between wall and foundation,
reveal the house leaning against the fence
like a tired horse, must be shifted back, else
we're weighing the world. We snake a chain
around a beam, crank with a come-along hooked
to a post, and coaxed to the point of breaking—
something gives—the whole house slides shuddering
into place, the arm comes to life, ascending
in levity, equilibrium restored.

On sale day, weights glide—slid along the balance-
beam—rising and falling upon the year. Flood and drought,
thick summer air, and bone-eating cold, come into account.
Things we needed and did without tell in flesh
as we part out groups—ten calves at a time—to chase
in through the gate, hold a moment, and weigh.

Ten more—

load by load, until no more to be found.
Cattle are bought and sold by the pound.

Voices

Another sleepless night passes as I sit
writing in the cool air of the porch,
exiled again to unsettling thoughts
of disease, family and money, disruptions
to our lives as the dream of spring is held
fast in a grip of unbroken drought, depleted
pastures and no promise of weather for weeks.
This should be May instead of March.

Somehow a lone frog voice issues softly
from the quiet, into the dark and as if waiting
for their cantor, a unison of congregants in trees,
amid leaf and bracken beside the dry pond answers
in creaking antiphony. The sound rises, spreads
its solace upon the land apprehending the gloom
and in this moment it is easy once again
to believe in things to come.

Shit

I stepped close to hold her tail, as they
told me to do, and Doc Lindsey,
up to his armpit inside, started raking
it out with his cupped hand—manure
spattering everywhere—and he spied
my cringe, ducking out of the line of fire,
and said, *Don't worry boy—*
It's clean til it hits the ground!

During the annual Florida Beef Cattle Shortcourse
at the University in Gainesville, Alan De Ramus,
professor of Agronomy from the University
of Louisiana at Lafayette,
came to tell us about cow shit.

Lights turned low, he presented slide after slide:
hard-packed heaped masses drying in the light,
or loose slurries and gruels steaming in early
morning legume pastures of the Southeast;
all projected on a large screen.

We saw diarrheas, constipations, and soft
amalgamations, the consistency of pancake batter.
Now that's what you want, he said. *If she's*
shittin' like that eating your grass,
you can't do another thing for her.

One winter, we crossed the brown pastures
on the north end of the ranch, nothing but frosted
grass, fence to fence, and all the cows gathered
in the corner, crying where they spent the night
waiting on us to come and let them move.
The field was cobbled in hard-made piles,
littering the ground everywhere. We opened
the gate, thinking where they're going is no better than
where they've been, but were grateful to send
them somewhere. And my father said, closing the gate
behind them, *Son, looks like they're shittin' bullets!*

Soul Lost

We rode with Rob and Tiffany out to John and Pam Vocelle's late yesterday afternoon to help them work their cows and have dinner afterward. It was a quiet evening in the enjoyable company of friends. I listened to an entire Gary Stewart album after our meal, falling asleep in a chair as I soaked in the music contemplating this strange, talented soul from the next town south and his beginnings playing and singing in the raucous exosphere of dank bar-rooms, *honkytonks,* and dives, and his ascent to some measure of Country Music stardom. He sang of *whiskey trips,* things gotten *out of hand,* and *callin' it quits,* from the eternal aspects of heartache and pain. We talked about him—how several months ago he killed himself after the loss of his wife and, earlier, his son, fulfilling his own dirges of trouble and despair. We can but listen, and wonder about all this. What is the Easter morning version of Gary Stewart? It is my prayer his soul scurried off to love more encompassing and intense than he could ever imagine. I pray he is home.

Folly

Waldo Sexton had already founded the first dairy in the county
starting with one cow, planted an 80-acre grove, caretaking
others, and set ten thousand trees in first planting. He *went to
farming* in these tropics where you *can put in three crops a year
and lose your ass in all three,* cleared rights of way from
lagoon to ocean and the A1A roadbed to the inlet on the barrier
island with a hand crew, mules, and grubbing hoes . . .

He would become president of seventeen corporations, co-found
the Indian River Citrus League and have the first Florida oranges
chemically analyzed. He'd construct a packing house, lay out a sub-
division, select vistas for the front nine holes of the Royal Park Golf
Course, organize the first county fair, breed guinea cattle, and three
new avocados. He started the Real Estate Board of Vero Beach,
built a hotel, three restaurants, a world-famous tourist attraction,
and, lastly, raised a mountain.

He had *four children,* he reported, and *only one wife,* but perhaps
foolishness, always there, came to full flower when he could not
ignore a challenge flung to the world by A.B. Nolan of Carlisle
Barracks, Pennsylvania, who claimed in an issue of *Nature Magazine*
he'd grown the largest elephant ear leaf in the United States,
including California, at fifty-four-and-a-half inches long. Waldo wrote
Nature to enter the "contest," reporting a *sixty-two-inch leaf.*

With no word, he wrote again, wondering if they *did not report
the size of my Elephant Ear to Mr. Nolan. If you did, he has restricted
his territory, because I certainly come within the Florida area
and since reading this article, I've gone out and checked up on the
growth for this year and I find the largest leaf I have is 54 inches
in width and 64 ½ inches long. I went to the expense of getting
a local photographer to take a picture. I trust you will advise
Mr. Nolan he still has a mark to shoot at.*

Dear Aunt Lee

Days we thought would not come for you are past, as we gather
with an abiding sense of your presence. There are a thousand
topics to cover, remembering you. First is about love and how its
stain spreads imperceptibly from the heart. We are a lucky people
of a fortunate land, given to certain affection and see ourselves
peculiarly different from those not knowing such love. You called
this the *Something Special City* and actually believed and helped
make it so. We owe you thanks for public beaches and parks, a
well-placed bridge, and unbroken view of the sky from any sector

of our county where, as a twelve-year-old, you and your lifelong
friends rode bicycles to the beach, swam, explored, fished and
messed about the river in boats, and tramped through hammocks
and sloughs. Who among us can say we've lived our whole lives in
the places we were born, and in so doing, found so much to love?
That rare attribute comes only seldom from the human condition,
and is to be prized like tomorrow's light upon our shimmering
boroughs of mangrove, and citrus, wherever they remain.

You did so much in your time women were not only not supposed
to do but simply couldn't, and always donned proper disguise—
your favorite perhaps the electrifying countenance of *One,* as my
grandfather would say, *who didn't know she couldn't* and like him
always possessed vision you were unable to keep to yourself that
likewise, included us all. We figured you invisible—by the ground
you covered on your paths through a male-dominated world,
intractable as the western marshes of the county, but truth is, no
radar has ever been fashioned that could keep track of you.

You sprung from the stock of what used to be termed an old-world family of merchants, born with the requisite acumen and impulses to succeed two lifetimes in business; beginning with your adolescent lemonade stand. The rest of your upbringing is historied in achievement. By all accounts you could take a man down when it was needed done and by your prowess and skill, should have been a golf or tennis professional, and were easily mistaken as such on more than one occasion as when asked for an autograph, happily signed your own name.

Your prodigy in business took on life of its own, a life you shared with your beloved Lucy, third on a list of most admired people, comprising Mother Teresa, Sandra Day O' Connor, and your dear mother. With a grub stake from Herschel Auxier and advice from such mentors as Dan Richardson, and E.G Thatcher, the two of you joined into business, and *Alma Lee's* the clothier came into being—one more place for that incipient *love* to manifest—where any child of the county could embark newly outfitted for the world. *That Alma Lee's store smell!* How it seeps from the creaking old pine floor of memory, and filled racks and shelves of the *everyday* in what we found and drew upon ourselves.

Uniforms, sportswear, formal apparel. You anticipated us with each fresh crop of clothes on buying trips—Atlanta to Miami—*Lucy had to pick the frilly things at the shows as it was well known you would have none of it.* And we arrived at the end of the long summer, our household budgets in tow; children and adults alike received with that twinkle in your eye, as a perpetual cold cup of coffee sat waiting on your desk, and you among us in that blessed familiarity, never forgetting a name or face.

You learned our sizes, knew what we would soon outgrow and
in turn, saw the city we'd one day exceed. It was a natural thing
for your love to bring you to public service, as it would anyone
wanting to keep the world a better place. You campaigned for and
won a seat, a woman's first, on the County Commission which
you held twelve years in consecutive election, in time serving
as chairman. And with the local politic grew your benevolence,
always perceiving us, working behind the scenes as you did in
business, in answer to the ways we'd change and grow. The list
of your philanthropies calls to mind Homer's catalogues

of ships in the Iliad: gardens and special lands, a lagoon, hospital,
colleges and schools, museums, libraries, a theatre, sports teams,
activity and learning centers, social and business organizations,
Not-for-Profit community boards and a youth orchestra for under-
privileged children. By your own ascendance you set supreme
example in advocacy of rights of women and further mentored,
supported and led them to new *places* in unparalleled fashion
of our hundred-year history as a city and two-hundred years as
a state. This was commemorated on the centennial of women's
suffrage by your induction into the Florida Women's Hall of Fame.

You became as a friend spoke of you, a *lovely older person*, mulled
into a fine varietal by your span of days. You were always publicly
fair, knowledgeable of *what was*, and handled differences with the
aplomb of a career diplomat. You were given the good sense to
choose your fights and knew what to do when things took a hard
turn. A beloved niece said: *Because she had faith, she always knew
the right things would happen. She was my hero and I was her star.
I would do anything she wanted me to do, because she told me
I could. I'm certain she believed in me like no one else, but I can
understand if everyone else she knew felt the same.*

What about romance? I asked one of her true intimates, who replied: *She had loves, and disappointments—who hasn't?* Yet one day something came to flower inside her and she chose to be married at last to the people and places of her *Something Special City,* and in that moment, became our bride.

Departure

Monday Week

The light has become a soft illumination of the distant field—
that lovely painting in which I've been privileged to stay
and someday die. A frog's staccato—solitary and clear—
says, *What are we to do today*, and his friend answers from
across the yard, bespeaking surety if not complaint;
in unison of peace and plight.

We are no different, once our hearts are driven from their hiding
places. There, is hope alike in what comes wending from his morning
"fiddle string" and even with a bad back, trepidation of war, corrupt
leaders, artistic struggle, and COVID's present visitation upon our
household—along with a coming week of work and strife—gratefully
I receive the day's new commission.

The pump in the yard switches on . . . and off—
                                        then another moment's quiet.

Poem of Edgar

There is a poem of Edgar to speak,
now he is no longer here communing
his poetry of fascination with the strangeness
and beauties of the world—
things he held in awe and gifted
back to us with tellings and art.

Circuses he ran off to were barely different
to him than the great novelty taking place
daily outside his door. The high wire and lofty
realms known only to *trapeezists* and *canoneers*,
were but commutations upon extended glimpses
of pattern on water, and color in the sky.

The fond voice of a neighbor, the consoling
whisper of his spouse, were an ongoing
benediction for life well spent considering
all things: mineral or blood, breathing
or staid, to be an extravagant
construct of magic.

From elephants to drumsticks, molten bronze
to the machinations of a well-made SLR,
he saw us contained by even as we comprise,
the exquisite miracle called the *Universe*,
every portion—of sweet devise,
and, the grandest piece of luck.

Dirge

I want to take the old way home
now your life has come to ruin.
We left you in the dark alone.

The story chills me to the bone
hearing I will lose you soon;
We used to take the old way home.

Now my heart is turning stone.
When I arrive you may be gone
passing through the dark alone

Sister of my blood and bone,
We barely have an afternoon,
I need to find the old way home.

Time for us has come and gone
they said, again, you'll leave us soon
to wander on your path alone.

How the pain has only grown
now your life has come to ruin.
I have to find the old way home
and follow through the dark alone.

Remains of Barney

There are none—he's disappeared as he arrived
through the slender air, affixing to our lives
as though we'd been acquainted a thousand years.
Athlete in a tuxedo, the black and white coiffure
of that elegant body—lithe, Orcan,
precocious as lightning.

Disappearance always his second art, practiced
upon four households, four cat food dishes set
out for him, he managed to empty daily,
keeping a presence, drowsing settees
windowsills and the daybed, in schedules
of philandering unbeknownst to any of us.

He leaves confusion in remain of whose he was
or who were his, and a certain levity in our sense
of lost visitation. He could circle the house entire
and rush one door having just been put out the other,
never failing to gain, when access was his goal
reinstatement in the household.

The algae-filled dish of rainwater is a disused
memento of his absence, four weeks passed.
We're certain something's happened, though we
claimed nothing could catch him, not coyote
nor traffic. In his late-night excursions from
barn to back door. His soft, persistent, three a.m.

paw thuddings, the destruction of my sleep. Ever
present, except when he wasn't, and ready any hour
for fawning caress and endless draughts of attention.
He imposed upon us like the seasons.
Better or worse, that I speak of him at all
yields to my own disbelief, and yet who would expel

Apollo from one's life once he moved in? Never drive
beauty from your door, should be the entreaty of
any cultivation, for it will leave soon enough on its
own. And he is gone whence he came, vanished
into the ether, and there's a vacancy,
in the abiding hostelry of our hearts.

RFK/RIP

Is it enough to say who came?
Marvelous crowds appeared trackside
along the route of the train.
But what are they good for now?
It was complained; as they gathered
in mourning, numb with disbelief,
frozen in despair of fresh evil
joined to the *common works of man.*

Twenty cars made up the cortege
a thousand aboard in stifling heat
of early June: a *disparate mélange
of family, friends . . . celebrities.* Manhattan
to Washington—taking twice as long
as it should: an eight-hour day.
*The food ran out, the water ran out,
finally the liquor ran out.*

The coffin rode in the last car; chairs
were brought from the dining coach
for a makeshift bier to lift it into view.
And she alone, her veiled head
resting against the casket, rosary
in her fingers. *I wasn't ready
to see that,* a witness said.
The train carried the remains

of our hope, said another.
I put my hand on my heart,
a woman remembered, saying,
*Who would we walk to the edge
of a track* and *stand there for* today?
Two million souls along the way—
arriving early, staying late,
some missing it by a moment.

Waving, saluting, kneeling, praying,
paying last respects. Thronged cities,
sparse countryside, lonely barrens,
all the siding a neighborhood—
over two hundred miles of them watching,
waiting, expecting, aching, forgoing meetings,
appointments, and schedules to be there.
Some had been shopping,

some left jobs, school, abandoned posts.
Some left home, some left their lives.
Windows flowed along clacking rails
past so many faces as to appear to the riders
they themselves were frozen, the world
rolling by. Faces of hurt, fear, passion,
and loss, and those present for the novelty
of it, out of curiosity, out of horror.

They carried flowers, flags and banners.
Homemade signs: *RFK/RIP,*
So-Long, and *We love you-Bobby.*
They held handkerchiefs, cameras, umbrellas,
purses, children, and pets. They held each other,
assembled in parking lots, open fields, under
bridges, crowded embankments, road
crossings. drainages, and backyards.

They were dressed up, uniformed, wore robes
and habits, bathing suits, diapers—high fashion
and homespun, shirtless and soiled. Firemen,
cops, hairdressers, car salesmen, and nurses.
A Cub Scout troop, entire baseball team,
marching bands, congregations, strangers,
nuclear families. Young, old, glamorous, destitute,
homely, wealthy, red, yellow, black, and white.

New York to Union Station. When they arrived,
the *moon hung heavy and full over the Potomac.*
At the Lincoln Memorial, they all sang
The Battle Hymn of the Republic; then
across the bridge into Arlington. *A light rain
had stopped.* Old friends, weary pallbearers,
trusted aides, and family champions stumbled up
the hill to the knoll to lay him beside his brother.

Only a marvelous country would have
dared *to have him,* taken his promise
to make us *a little better* than we were.
His mettle—*not strong, not weak:*
somewhere between a blade of grass,
and *finely-honed . . . steel.*
His *mild and magnificent eyes,*
now accustomed to the dark.

Midway

On the last leg of a homebound
flight, we lift off the dreary,
frozen tarmac of Midway,
climb through a dense ceiling

to open sky, high above a vast
shining scrim of soft batting
reaching beyond limits of sight.
The harmed, misgiven world

asleep below like a lost
child in its coverlet.
One could almost wish
we'd never come down.

Libélula

On the way home from the barn, I noticed a large dragonfly glittering in the road, struggling where he'd been hit. His head was barely attached, hanging by a *central* cord. I picked him up and his grip came firm upon my fingers, affixing as if to announce he was very much alive in his nearly beheaded state. I brought him home thinking I might draw him and as I drove along, I tried to replace his head to his body. But it only fell away swinging on that tenuous string. He rustled his wings incessantly, though he'd lost all capacity for flight and was difficult to loosen from my hand when I came onto our porch to see about repairing him. It wasn't possible to replace his head in any fashion, so I left him on a soft cloth on the table where he quietened, the luminous emerald lantern of eyes still strung, laying beneath. I returned to work thinking he could at least be at peace and wondered when and what for him death should be. . . .

Later, I visited my wife's mother in the nursing home after she fell and was there recovering. On the way out through the long hall, I came upon a woman I knew, strapped in, clutching the arms of her wheelchair. Many years ago, I did a painting for her. I used to see her at the store, but never knew she'd come to this—held fast and alone—as she raged there, all her thoughts missing.

World without Odis

Before you died, I wondered if there could be a world without you.
Time passes and more of you returns to me in thoughts of your
mannered voice pouring softly like molasses from a jar. You'd call
my name in salutation when I answered the phone, *Now Sean!*
and in turn answer my calls, *Hello Odis* . . . after Nancy, or later,
Mae Peck fetched you to the line. What became of your trappings
your garage and sheds half full of tools and fixtures of your life,
the other with curios from my grandfather's *Epic* he pleased himself
to enjoin and send home with you, filling your spaces after his over-
flowed? Have the small, ordered rooms and low ceiling that always
astounded me with a different scale of living upon entering your house
disappeared with your life?

And your congeries of half-broken black men, gleaned from your
neighborhood to abet you: Gene, always lame, always at hand; Big
Ernie, all crosstie and rail who'd get mad if the work got easy; Shorty,
bantam-weight before his bout with time rendered him wordless;
and Bubba, rotund and wise in his blue, crushed velvet flat cap, air of
the country club about him, foil-wrapped bait of barbequed coon
stowed for repast upon heroic tasks. Have they joined he *spotty shell*
and marl banks they dug into setting drain tiles, or moved a last giant
slab of wood, worthy of King Arthur's court? Are they still in a bind
holding a huge piece of wrought iron to fasten in place, or vanished
as the *palm trees withering like blades of grass* before your machine
gun, island to island in the South Pacific?

———

I know part of your world keeps in your absence because I helped
bear you to your grave. Mine, the only white hands chosen with
a final remnant to carry you: Joe Morgan, Nate Jackson, Renny
Beachum, Cedric Johnson, and Sam Pickens. Your silver crypt shines
in hard light of the ridge north of Gifford, where rank and file reside
with *Uncle Eddie*, *ML*, *Speedy*, and *Saul* in a final precinct of bones
of the great souls in my grandfather's employ. You always said you
were from *Orange Lake*, and it lent levity and *otherness* to your bearing.
There was intelligence and mystery cast in you others took in awe.
You were wary of frightful things—never caught out *deep sea* with
Moxey on his leaky boat, no late-night excursions to the *Green Leaf*
on Saturday where Mosely got rolled on an inside job saying, *They*
put a drug in my drink—they body-slammed me!

You were domestic and gainly as fishing worms raised in boxes of
dark soil, sold from your shed, pulled in two to grow and double the
return; hens in elegant coops you built gave endless supply of eggs.
Your garden thrived in the poorest substrate of the county where you
keep estate this moment, where a *world without Odis* parlays into un-
requited emptiness. You learned masonry, *stole it* by your account,
laboring for *Nick the Greek* as he set the local, brittle lime rock into
walls, benches, and fireplaces of our residences and buildings, peering
wryly askance as you labored, mixing and toting concrete and stucco,
and soon he swore by you, enamored of your poise and energy as we'd
all become. You were my Grandfather's right arm, and to this day your
carpentry engenders a vernacular in every facet of our lives.

And now this world of no more buckets of bluefish left on our door-
step from all-night fishing trips to the inlet, no further tales of
Obechobee and other destinations of high adventure; nor further
account of the *tombic bomb*, you witnessed and retold, surviving to
return home and thread the racial incongruities of postwar America.
You were stout as *mud* you mixed, boards you cut, blocks you laid,
and smart as those you did it for—building two extra houses on your
tiny lot to become a landlord and upwardly mobile. There is the story
of when you were sent to jail for passing a bad check and summoned
my Grandfather to make bail, to whom, arriving with admonishment
and scorn, you said:

It wasn't bad, they just kept it too long.
When he replied, *Why didn't you spend the night, they'd have let you
out in the morning?*
You said, *I just does better out of jail.*

Oh—to see your brown Dodge truck again, pulling into my yard,
laden with family treasures you felt I should have, ruining my day
in your steady, unfaltering passages of story and dissertation and
have time slip down that hourglass, full of the sweet cane syrup
of your voice, for now you've gathered those who kept this world
with you and gone to greater tasks: slab and mortar, iron and bell,
in a farther realm and leave us to know your kind no more.

Dilemma

A family of mice moved
into a leftover
sack of grain
on the backdoor stoop,

chewed a ragged, quarter-sized
hole in the end
of the bag where
they now reside.

First thing this bright winter morning
I have cattle
to feed, tenants
to send packing.

Departure

The bony old cow in the set-aside
field, one eye blind, swollen shut.
We'd have shot her but for lack
of a gun as she lay panting.
We fixed a waterline in the far
pasture, rather than fixing her
for death, and passed by once
more on our noon break.

I brought water in the early afternoon
meted a small sum of feed
with doubt she'd eat, found her
curled into a dark shell of herself,
forlorn embryo between worlds.
I patted her and felt her shallowing breaths,
wishing her on her way.
My mother died like that.

Lament

The wooden slab helps one recall and forget the tree,
its squared mien a complete oddity to nature:
frozen river of grain, portal you stare
into but not through. Knots here and there—
haphazard buttons of a garment—once origins
of boughs shorn and left fallen on a ruined
forest floor. Yet hoary shapes haunt
this remaining form, emblem of what
is done when we have things our way
as the new clear-cut lot along the highway.

Auto Zone Coming says the sign to vacant,
foreboding space where once flourished
a breathing green riot of my childhood.
Felled, shredded, hauled away;
obliteration I lived long to behold
now spoken of as way of the world.

In Yonder Fields

In yonder fields they never know
where they've been sent to graze and grow.
To stand beneath unblinking skies
and mark their place with keening cries
with never anything to know.

They were here short days ago
and watched the mornings come and go,
loved and were loved and sent away
in yonder fields.

Let your wonder come and go,
there's never anything to know—
that whole dark night the mammies cry
and stand beneath an empty sky
to stay until their voices die;
with never anything to know
in yonder fields.

The Wedding Dance

Yesterday Morning

I coaxed you out with me to go open a gate and let the cattle move
and we found the pasture filled with swallows, winging in trajectories
of near misses, steep swoops—perilous courses bringing them close—
so it seemed wire was strung across our path in grand,
disappearing hoops.

At the hem of hoof and horn as the cattle stirred on our approach,
white birds arose, like a thousand prayer flags filling the sky.
And we drove to them in the distance every time they landed, to see
it happen again; swallows always just ahead—candle-wicking the air
so we forgot the cattle and the gate and got back home a little late.

All Things Are Found in All Things

for Charles Wright

The road,
trees are printed on its surface from dripping
leaves, unswallowed dew in the sky—
between branches for only a moment,
a pale, colorless stone, the moon.

Is it there because we are here? Or do we live by
what we see through branches in the sky,
as we stand in the damp morning on trees
sketched by dew, fallen from leaves above
the road.

Lenten Airs

. . . sorrowful as the early days of Spring
—Rilke

I

At first hint of rain:
a vagrant breeze cuts the dark—
every frog complains!

II

By these ill-blown whiles
the new morning spider-work
only full of holes.

III

How the feeder swings
in remain of the buntings
and all wanting things.

IV

O' fresh-tainted breeze!
And already a plenty
of orphans to feed.

And Now Our Aged House

has run its course,
disgorging children into the universe.
How many days since the Certificate
of Occupancy was granted and into time,
we within this space, embarked upon life
with no map, no instrument—
save our wish, and blind intent.

And where once in the yard, we stood
beside blonde, tightly bound stacks of wood,
the fragrance of a forest misplaced,
abroad, and soon walls, framed, braced—
and risen to sudden interruption of light
in the place we call our life.

Walls now staid upon an unblemished
green pudding, formed, and fleshed,
by mason's jook and trowel. Smoothed
and cured, set in motion in one dappled
afternoon, the long ascent—rafter
by angle, bird mouths and header—

to the ridge: apex of our determination.
Month by man, minute by nail, a rendition
of where the world stays still.
Our *inside* has come of it.
But time insists, the hard angles of living
set in days, tell on us and everything.

Opening joinery, catching windows,
racking doors, points of resistance grown
weary, the world finds ingress
through roof and wall, mortar and glass—
rustling in the closet, creaks in the stair,
and mouse-inveigled very air,

parsing threshold and latch to be with us here,
with heat and damp, cousins of rain and fire.
And how within its own footstep, a place can walk,
and go nowhere, whereby fences no longer make
sense, storm-felled shade—laurels that once showed us
where to live, now replanted in maple and cypress

dug up from the fallows across the road—
and like tomorrows have multiplied
and filtered familiar light into old rooms
and additions. A new porch which seems
now to have always been, constructed
upon damage, between tempests outlasted.

Leaking valleys, darkened space, confused
electricity, the old: disrupted, and improved,
an outdoor hearth and terrace with half of heaven
to roof away, after we danced and to be certain,
star-gazed three years. The summer chimney
nested with swifts, arriving from the sky,

a wayward smoke, halting all immolation
into early autumn when they fly, *heaven
knows where*. Time is spoken in all,
and on farthing breeze a soft caterwaul—
in place of quiet: the new neighbor's
cattle grazing old eastward acres.

Now land ditched and dried in surrounds
of lost citrus lands, banished sounds,
and the next world has its way with us
as a flooding river flowing past.
We remain people of our settling and stay,
for wings to find and carry us away.

The Mast

for Claude Wilkinson

The ancient oak has waited long to speak, sending
admonishment or laughter ringing this season
as the mast strikes the roof in ongoing repartee.

Hot little nouns drop, turn verb at the last moment—
clatter, and pound, any hour of day or night
assailing at times our dreams.

Spoken in particles or whole broken branches filled
with leaves and corns, they arrive like missives
from the reaches so we worry *the sky really is falling.*

All gone unsaid between us and our taciturn neighbor
litters the terrace in daily memos of arboreal matter—
and as we are blind to complication overhead also

do we step unaware out of doors upon the transcript
in Braille: our erasures and redactions given
with broom and blower but there's more to come,

always something needs said that takes all season
so we might wonder that any peace keeps between
us the rest of the year.

How long—in these terms—the infant mango delays
fruit and bloom, or budding guava, her ascent on shaded
rungs while we barely know when to hold our tongues!

So, the wise, mysterious anestrus of nature, strains
that birth every other year, post-vernal appearances
of spider, dauber, and swallow, the locust's

episodic wakening, certain seeds after centuries
or flush of toadstools from one kind of rain but no other,
each for *a time to every purpose under heaven.*

The Wedding Dance

At the fond celebration of a young couple's
wedding and an evening worn on, the DJ
called for a spouse's dance. He put on a single
as we assembled, and soon the most recently
joined had to stop as he shouted *a year!* Several
left at *two,* when he continued his count:
three, four, five, and the next, and the next.

Music changed several times in the course:
eight years, ten, twelve—as in a game of chairs—
they departed. Another song and we danced on,
fifteen, twenty. How was it we were still there
holding each other in the unseemly dank,
small-town moment, swaying along
in the blaring kitsch of an awful soundtrack.

Twenty-five, and three remained. *Thirty* trimmed
us to two. *Thirty-three, thirty-four, thirty-five,*
and we danced time away, each number another
step, *thirty-six* and *seven*—we knew it soon over.
Thirty-eight years and *we* left the floor.
The last couple—it wasn't even close—
finally quit at *forty-six!*

Noise

To his wife's chagrin, he left his music playing
out on the porch, from the early morning, past day
and through the night. *It quiets the birds in the yard*
she would say, *and sends them away so I can't hear
them anymore*, or, *It gives me the creeps to go by
the door on my way to bed and hear music playing.*

But, he answered, *it drowns the crickets in my
head—singing all the time—please don't begrudge
what keeps me unmindful of that sound.*
And in sleeplessness when he'd go out and sit
beneath a lamp at the end of a table to write, with
music issuing softly,

two owls in the treetops would open their monkey calls
to one another, talking to him and he to them in mimic,
or in the wee hours out in the pasture where could be heard
the plaintive cries of calves in answer to their mother's
lowing on occasions the herd came up in the dark
to camp close to the fence and listen.

And certain times, a thousand coying yelps would rise in answer
to a distant siren, or the train, pounding softly through town,
the damp, crepuscular air, an eardrum receiving the *Branden-
burg Concertos, Flamenco Sketches,* or *Suites for Solo Cello,*
and Eva Cassidy or Peggy Lee, shrill and alive to all things vested
in the quiet of the land, out beyond the handprints of sound.

Lost and Found

I turn pages of an old book to find
a misplaced folded sheave;
take out and open to a poem in blue
ink—four stanzas about you—
and I wonder when it was written.
In your hand on the verso,
                            with the same pen:

Mop & Glow,
as if you'd just begun a list for the grocer.
I ponder scrawled and dispossessed words
to whom they belong—abandoned
at times like orphan calves to fend
for themselves,
                        I read:

As You lift your arms in explication,
I divine that softness
wrought through your body to beckon
again to my hands to fondle and kiss.

I imagine your alpine region, its verges
and alluring crevasses
to visit and explore
in opportune traverses.

And you ask for a hank of paper
towel to blotter and dry lettuce,
for your salad, ridiculous
little requisite of order,

yet I would spend the world without
regret and gladly ruin
all peace to see you content,
humming to yourself, alone.

Empty Nest

She brought home a jigsaw puzzle
to solve our days.
There is a well-
known, time-worn way

to do this, like learning to kiss:
pouring pieces
on a table
turning them all

up to search for the straight edges
so you can set
out a border.
Use the picture

on the cover to find your way
and soon you will
remember all
the shapes you try

here and there in the emptiness.
Hold and shed them
like cards. In time
as the spaces

begin to fill, misgivings soon
fly away. For
better or worse,
we work alone.

Pieces join—images come forth
—figures appear:
a proud caliph
with shouldered spear,

narrowed eyes, and bright, plumed turban;
a corpulent
old oliphant
decked in garlands,

paisley duvet, young dowager
aboard, portaged
through a dazzling
garden. Orchids,

peafowl, and butterflies surface
and piece by piece
sadness begins
growing within.

We imagine our work ending,
puzzle complete,
and only then
taken apart.

Everything put back and stowed in
the box, soon to
be forgotten,
thrown out or lost.

Hand,

underside still young,
transacting, dog
of mind, grasp of work—
hammer, pliers, pencil—
ready.

Top like the moon—
aged, wrinkled,
rim of man—
headed toward
dark,

one foot in hell,
other on a banana peel.

Who are we but
battered ones?
Ragged tabernacles,
taking time on the chin—
in use or demise, all
matters at hand.

Pictures of the Early Gods of Our Adolescence

Now we barely know ourselves
from images circulated online
of past parties and revelries.
To recall this boy, that girl, sometimes
bystanders a key to puzzle names,
recount the notorious with their great
sobriquets: *Crab, Woot, Studley*, and *Worm*,
defamation turned acclaim in time
for those we discipled to,
canonized, and adored.

Many no longer among us:
Jeff Snyder and Kenny Price,
early gone; Donnie in rehab,
Albert Valdez lost last month; *Whitehead*
(Randy not Steve), long ago graved.
Wraiths, desolate as beauty, remaindered
in these snaps, this quaint technology,
as from a great struggle, a final offing glimpse—
seen through a mirror dimly,
but then face-to-face.

How Strange We Live So Long to Know

How strange we live so long to know;
The little days, the midden arcs
of time through each year's half-dreamt
joy and ever-present half-dread harm,
as season into season flows
upon an everlasting dark.

Our homely residence of flesh
We strangely live so long to know,
as nestlings from a honeyed hive,
to strangelings of when we propose
to seek and bind ourselves to love
in fear, if only then to die.

To feel the swallow in the drown
from fallows of the days' compend
we strangely live so long to know;
the summer languor, rising wind,
the soil's swell of fulsome leaven
which soon the firmament will thin.

In flight along from passing thought:
a helpless race on frozen legs that
runs toward sleep and breathless end,
we strangely live so long to know
upon the path through troublous light,
all toward a long and deathless night.

And soon a darkening descends
and gathers in our kith and kin,
to give us to ourselves alone—
amid the places we have been,
we've lived so long to strangely know
and find a peace our kind bemoans.

From silence did we come and grow
toward infant light and worldly din
and learned with breath we'd taken in,
to make the dark an olden friend
as time would have us meet again
and live so long to strangely know.

Portals

Sonnet on a Glass Snake

with a Line from Derek Walcott

Already shorn of length, he's in the road—
a shining apparition of the world
that made him, same as the lissome sables,
maudlin thrush, heedless, infernal mistral
sent to chastise the fields and brown the brush.
Difficult to handle as oil-soaked ice,
he's not a snake, nor made of glass, yet
legless, benign in danger; will not bite;
gives a piece of himself, to save you both.
Flees like a word, or name not coming forth
from the somnolent realms of the tongue
trying to fasten on everything it moved from.

Only late finds a door to the alleys of grass,
and like summer wind, flies away at last.

Hillside Equipment Auction Yard
outside Dothan, Alabama

I'm the wretch the song's about.
    —Bumper sticker seen on a truck driving through Alabama

A soft breeze mingles in the teeth
of an ancient harrow set beside stacked
stock panels and piles of rusted field fence;
falters upon a mass of engine blocks
submerged in visqueen like boulders in a
hard flowing mountain stream as a frozen
silence pervades the iron redoubts of the
hillside equipment auction yard.

There is a forlorn pause among disparate
machines hauled, driven, or dragged into places
they seem remaindered from a wayward carnival.
Aromas of fresh paint and grease confuse the
apparition they comprise, cast from distant
fields into glittering rows as stood the Spartan
army among the dunes in early morning light,
awaiting the trumpet's toll.

For sale on the morrow says the sign: tractors
of every make and model: dozers, loaders, graders,
backhoes and excavators, and spread beyond
their fantasy power upon the compound in descension
like the social ordering of a small-town cemetery,
the accessory dreams of agricultural invention:
combines and balers, buckets and spreaders,
Adam's cure—nearly nonsensical in the problems
of its fashioning—monuments to simple, ugly hope.

And you pass by, imagine yourself traversing the aisles,
searching at first your own emptiness for what isn't there.
Wanton remembrance arises in bruised-knuckle disdain
of the relic grain-drill with jammed seed tubes, frozen bearings,
and missing or broken springs, twenty years out of calibration
calling to you like the sirens from the rocks. Eighteen small birds
suddenly pass overhead in perfect formation, outpacing the air.
Mindlessly, you take them in—how they seem to know better
than you and your kind, where they should be going as they fly.

You're still 800 miles from home, full of allure of things
you were never meant to have, thankful you'll miss the auction,
any auction by sheer gravity of departure, leaving it behind
to the *sons of men*: dream-laden, addled, miserly, speculative,
and outright fools—yea the fools or everyone starves. You hurry
along, safe on your way knowing they will appear tomorrow
evening at the appointed hour, neighbors a thousand miles away.
All, little less than gods.
                    Their land, little more than graves.

Ars Poetica, Obstetrics, Painting, and the Rough Draught

It's like helping a calf to be born—poem-writing,
and if you believe in fate, perhaps you believe
such things already exist and only need deliverance.

There are the tools and dilemma to work against—
stillbirth always an imminent possibility, poem
in mind like a lamb in its mother's womb,

helped out with *warm oil and monkey-delicate*
fingers, legs righted—front first—streamlined
as a diver entering water, or a poem, the world.

Socrates said he followed in the family profession
of *midwifery, knew the pangs of labour and the*
bringing forth of something within.

Much like the interlude on a bright morning during
calving season—set up in the landscape to paint,
supplies unloaded, easel open and I notice a heifer

seeming in trouble, labor not progressing. I secure
the site and drive over to her, manage to catch and tie
her to a tree, crawl to her backside with a hay-string

in my teeth, and, making do, fashion two thongs
to catch the protruding legs. The *pull* is hard, so
I turn a palm stick into a handle for a better grip

And like an incontrovertible fact, he arrives
whole, blinking-eyed, rough-draught ready
to turn loose into a world from which he came.

Plea

*And he told them a parable that they ought always to pray
and not lose heart.*
                    —Luke18:1

An evening has passed, and a young cow is still crying
among the herd this morning like the widow in the Bible
who wouldn't leave an ill-tempered judge alone. And though
the judge neither *feared God nor regarded man*, he relented,
annoyed to at last attend what was unsettling her.

And so I've ridden out into the pasture to see what could be
the matter: did she misplace her calf as my wife might've left
her purse at the theatre? Or perhaps he's departed—tooth
and claw in pursuit—to the stars, as she'd have us believe
in her present anguish. There's nothing to find amid the indolent

drove, no tell-tale tuft, track, nor bleat to color the winsome
air. So, her pet grief goes unanswered, insufferable, while mist
has risen in the distance, grown upon itself to cover a world
it brings to our door, whispering onto dripping eaves,
rattling in the downspout, the earth's own soliloquy.

Our Rivers Are Hiding

Our rivers are hiding in the ground, and to trace
them to source, is a passing through the narrowed
auricles and ventricles of an ancient heart.
Seething through beds of marl and hollows
in rock, a true remain of the dark; robbed
from its beginning after late autumn ablution,
miserly spring to creep like blood from
a healing wound.

In wakenings of the tropics, months later
comes a sluicing from the borrows of heaven
when rivers are everywhere, driving out of the land
on old bedded courses in habit of erosion and
bioturbation, as if a frenzied animal turned
against its favorite peace to an open place
in escape to the slow halt of lagoon and
final sea.

And waters finally rise, mingle mid-step of root
and knee in slough-bound verges at the bottom
of breath where snail and hellbender crawl. Crimson
eggs purl spalted limbs; epiphyte and moss ceil
the mesic bog—sanctum whose extremities tear like
cloth against the world. And only after falling from
its hard portion does flowing resume, find sanction
with the creeping tide.

Once we disturbed an old water cow there, lodged mid-
stream as we paddled beneath moon and flowering vines,
wakened what the world had drowned in itself, thing
whose first name is Fear. She exploded, nearly swamping
us as she fled; the surprise not yet worn away half a life
later. We've heard the *slappy* mullet, felt the rivering
amble and know the draining reaches beyond brazen
gates, where ditches were long ago laid, steam-dug

on miled centers to unclasp the damp from its headland,
with uplands left to settle and farm. All the while the hold
depletes, disappears from places there will be no more
river, disappeared as if poured from a glass—each moment
an abandoned thought—the flowing, irrevocable wisdom
of water in a human-fated land.

A Suite in Minutes

I
David in Florida

Wordlessly, he consigns to fate
with a slaughter
lamb's dispassion
soft in his face

Lithe, skinny-dipping in the harsh,
tropical sun
whose burn may come
before the crush

of giant's sword and spear descends.
In listless stone
he stands alone,
to spell the end.

II
David's Penis

At the thigh's lovely conjunction
with abdomen
whereon angels
might hang apples—

were he a tree, there, his sallow
man-fruit beneath
a curly blonde
escutcheon—

utile—and set between marble
creases put where
every shepherd
crafts his fleeces.

III
His Scrotum

In their graceful asymmetry
David's gonads
hold the mind's hand,
soften wryly

into place where chisel, rasp, and
unearthly grasp
yield such gentle
cosmology.

Only geniuses and gods in
fashioning cods,
follow the way
of living clay.

IV
David's Navel

Of all sweet hollows in the flesh:
belly buttons
did not Adam
nor Eve possess.

With the touch of fingers on his
lover's face did
the sculptor use
a whetted blade

to carve the alabaster plain,
and raise no pain,
beyond his lone
adoration.

Bright Future

This moment, the future stops eating the past.
Starting today, we plough back the highways
into rubble whence they came, decree
a world tied together with memory:
Henceforth, no need to hurry here or there
for anywhere will be everywhere.

We've come to our senses—set a new course.
Wagons from the city have returned, horse-
drawn, laden with huge watermelons, picked
and taken the day before as out-of-work
eminent domain lawyers (suits shucked in court)
follow the dray-teams, unloading fruit.

Steadily they go, disgorging sweetness,
while boardrooms close, directors disperse
into planting crews soon sent around
while all the minutes are piled and burned.
The wagons lighten with every step—as
tomorrow grows smaller in homely progress.

Holes

Holes remember our way,
through gates, over roads and open ground:
traverses where they're painfully found—
how in the mind, a good wrenching stays
—to ever thus, be driven around.

Some so deep, they're hidden,
grassed over and like traps
forgotten;
made by creature, machine,
and the years' errant hands.

They keep like lies not questioned,
questions unanswered;
as a huge wallow in the far pasture
on the bank of an old ditch-section.
I didn't ask my father,

and the story never told—
how it came to be there
—in all our sixty years.
He and the truth are at rest, as holes
remain and endure.

Leavings

first thing

Green tell-tale piles
steam the morning glare,
where each arose and stood;
all breathing things afire
at least a while,
everything burning good.

———

Done in pearl,
quilted on air
with silken thread—
in an upper square
of field fence panel—
a glistening web.

———

A new-found flora,
swarming fresh damps
gobbets of spittle
from sucklings and mammies.
Heaven's diaspora
or hunger's expel?

Portals

Over here—place all things sudden:
                —B H Fairchild

Fetching a herd yesterday, we came upon a carpenter's square
rusting in the grass—bounced off the buggy and missing quite a
while. How severe and strange its hard angle in that setting.

Little, half-grown bull calf, growling softly as he walks the fence
line, posturing, jousting on occasion through the wire at other
calves, in full authority of his preeminence and discontent. To be
that certain!

Returning east down the lane—the morning bright unroofed our
distant barn.

Dog's great day: everything agreed with him, tail wagging,
euphoric, pouring himself through the hands of the crew in the
barnyard as we swapped stories waiting on the Vet to arrive and
preg-check the heifers. Half a day later, he's dead: rolled over and
killed by a truck slowly backing out.
When is our great day?

Out of the blue, sudden flash of lightning—thunderous boom—and
we all rush under the cover of the work shed not knowing our
ultimate safety there, yet one must go somewhere!

The leaning post—gate drags the ground one morning after the
other. Wrong from the start, whole fence line in collusion, and
it seems we must tear the world apart to make it better and that's
why it's only been thirty years.

I hung my hat on the Moses cow's horns when she came up snorting
as I "reeled in" her calf. She occupied herself the rest of the
moment getting rid of the hat while I tagged and turned him loose.

Then, there's a pelican overhead, soaring above the cow pens,
something the eye gathers in but mind can't place.

We stopped feeding the first-calf heifers January 26th. The next day, they fill the empty corner of the pasture by the gate, waiting in a large, expectant mass, crying at the sight of me going by in the buggy. Now that pang in my heart.

Sad thing. I found 206-91 heaped against a pine tree as I was moving the herds. I first assumed calving difficulty—perhaps one hung up in her, invisible, but in the calf book found she'd calved months ago. Then I figured struggle, an elderly cow can sometimes get hung in a wallow, unable to get her feet beneath her, displaced like a boat at low tide and as such, can drown [volume and contents of her rumen heaved upon her lungs, stifling her]. But she was sitting up cow-fashion on a mound, no sign of trouble, pawed ground, or stacks of manure behind. I brought Old Boss to see her. On approach, her calf there at her side, waiting for her to get up. He left crying as we drew close. Old Boss couldn't tell why she died. On our way home driving across barren winter landscape, I said: I think she got tired of this hard-assed, forsaken world and just decided to quit.

Frosted morning. Winter is a corporation that bought up all the land.

Coldest morning of the year and a clutch of egrets in the northern-most pasture of the ranch, strangely hunkered down, sheltering together in smut-grass clumps out of a stiff wind, basking in the sun, to warm up before going out to work.

Aloft today in a soft, misting rain is the sound of the interstate: dull ruckus of trucks, chirring tires, and constant whoosh-roar of traffic, as if an invisible highway were suddenly running through the pasture out across the way.

Walter Carlton earmarking three heifers John Durham bought from us. The grasp of his hand made the profile, shaped the ear as he swiftly sliced. Little pieces cut out (as if of felt or cloth) still litter the ground after men, cattle, truck and trailer, and whole day are gone.

Out this day to address again questions in my art, trying to make headway on a long, narrow (3' X 5') painting started a while ago and of course since I began around the end of the year, there's been quite a shift of light and shadow, changes that tempt me to ditch everything and start over. I'm compelled to move ahead, hurry outside, to the surface and get down to the *touches*, i.e. glazes, and nuance. Today the wind is a hindrance, as always when the year is so early. There seems a buffeting from nature's indecision: season, wind, and light. I feel old and set in my ways—yet my art is also young, unpracticed, suffering an internal wind. I can but stand in my life, as upon a rocky seaside shoal, and dwell beside an ocean of things unknown. Perhaps something will lift and carry me through. As always, it falls to heaven as to what sort of painter I am to be.

I think of Robert Baird's face—returning to the ranch eight years after buying two Brahman cows from us. He lost one that day on his way home. He said: She never got up after she went down. We called and offered him a free heifer, learning he recently lost eleven cows from a lightning strike. Old Boss picked the best one in the pen for him before he arrived. Robert walked up carrying a baby. We shook hands, barely remembering one another, but he still had a forthrightness and dignity we saw in him before. I pointed to the heifer saying, We just branded her for you. He smiled and said, Wow—She's pretty! As we were loading, I confessed to him how badly we felt hearing he'd lost the cow the first time and now the lightning strike. He said, Yeah, you expect one to die every once in a while, but to lose them all in one moment—that was really tough! He seemed happy as he left, carrying that smile along with him. It's been difficult to feel good these days.

April nearly over. Suddenly, I recall a gate left open for convenience of watering trees, six trips in—four tree-waterings each trip. There is a break in our Eden—gate forgotten, thing we cannot let happen. There are rules of paradise, violate them and you may come to know how God feels. Whiskey, cigars, lust, greed: more gates left open. They mimic nature, (*human* nature?) and yet tonight at dark, perfume in the air, jasmine! The month of tomfoolery draws to a close.

I took Julia out on the land east of our yard and performed the
Blessing Ceremony we learned on the Father/Daughter retreat we
recently attended with our church. It was a beautiful evening, her
eyes green as Korean jade. I spoke to her and remembered
Sharon's eyes the morning we were wed in the pasture. I said to
her: Julia, I bless you, and pray for you a beautiful life and will
do anything I can to make sure you have one. I told her to look
east at the rising moon, and the colored land and sky to the west
and remember this moment and place so one day she might come
here again and think about me when I'm no longer in this world.

Today the baby geese no longer fit through the chain link fence
of the coop. It took one day (they were already out yesterday
morning as I was opening the door to the coop.) This morning all
four—inside—waiting.

Vision from afar: Vultures in a lightered tree—seen on a morning
excursion across the west side of the ranch—huge, black, ominous
leaves filling bare limbs: neither rain nor season will change their
color nor bring their disappearance.
They are middlemen of this world.

We took a moment this morning (at my wife's prompting) to
become God's creatures together again. (Hell, I said, the Boss Man
is away, kids are farmed out, and mother is laid up in the hospital,
how can we waste such opportunity?) I left the house afterward,
rearranged—empty of thought—a tingling in my spine. How
wonderful to have been Adam, tasting Eden each morning to
fritter away the day, assigning and calling things by name. Yet I
would have not failed in bringing about his same fate—of this I
am certain.

Back to work. . . .

The day is sullen, sky overcast before sunrise. Perhaps we're at
summer's midpoint today (something changes imperceptibly each
of these days). That said, I was astounded at the white, hot light
in the west two evenings ago. There's a feeling in the air as days
pass by—heat, powerful as it is—of some other thing arriving.
Just like the seasons, we are not indelibly here. We set conditions
of what follows as did our forebears before they even knew of
us, if ever they did. What are we making for those to come, in
this world, we think belongs solely to us?

A hen seems to be destroying (intentionally or by accident) every
chick that hatches in the nest. These misshapen little creatures
come forth—barely free of the egg—to each have their entrails
pecked and pulled out through their cloacas by the hen, so they
soon die. That a manure-caked egg from an ignorant, persistent
hen could be a portal into this world is amazing in itself—not to
mention her strange proclivities! Aside from this, it seems one
would have to travel in a spaceship to be here, follow long,
circuitous passageways, and climb up and down stairs as on a trip
into the Louvre or from JFK's terminal to arrive in the Imperial
City. But it all begins beneath a hen and in this case, a deranged one.

Weaning night, just back from the barn after checking the calves.
The moon is but an eye suspended in the head of a large, bird-like
cloud, its entire mass, brightly lit, flying across the sky in strange
formation until breaking free, the world suddenly even brighter. I
pulled into the "shade" of the yard, got out and heard cattle
crying in the distance on my way to the house, figured it was
going to be a long night, which it was.

Rain! It began yesterday, continued all night, looms large today.
That drowning of all sound in the downpour on the roof: so rare
to this moment of the year when we never know it's coming or
disappearance. It may stay thirty minutes, or thirty days and make
us rue the moment we ever wished for it—yet how welcome and
comforting this morning.

Looking into the dish of acid to watch the image etch into the plate. It is exciting to watch bubbles rising out of cracks that comprise the drawing, see its conventions in contour and modeled form become fixed after seeming so tenuous as mere scratches in a film of tar and wax. My first impulse is always to overdo, etch the hell out of them, let the images deeply engrain. Leave the roast in too long, trust that love takes care of itself, and oh—to find out you're wrong!

I'm worried I made a cow sick with my paint. Tuesday I was working in the heifer's pasture, left my easel standing in a perfect, shady place as I left to fetch something from the buggy and returned to find lick-marks across the painting. I'd used Flake White in passages to lighten the sky. Is this enough lead to harm a cow? There's a young, second calf heifer out there, now in a malaise—bloated, seemingly feverish. She won't go through the gate to join the others and won't graze. It could be something else (could be a hundred things!), but I have a terrible feeling I've killed my cow with art.

Intense realization of love toward my mate last night, laying together in bed, nodding in and out of slumber (both of us nearly in the realm of dreams, yet how vividly notions come from there.) In little, ongoing wakenings, I held and kissed her, stroked her soft skin and all goodness of life seemed to embody that moment.

My ancient, red 263-03 cow got down in a ditch and we couldn't get her out. We drove her the full length several times, hoping each time she'd reach the end and climb out. Twice she tried an ascent, failed only to turn around and head back the other way, slogging through a half a mile each time. She seemed to be losing strength each trip. We cut and cleared tree limbs, graded the bank with shovels into a kind of ramp hoping to make for her an easier climb. We got her close one last time, put a lariat on her and tried pulling, but she sank to her knees and we knew we'd soon kill her. So, we quit—left her there, gates open—took lunch and put her out of our minds. She was among the herd, grazing when we returned.

Ultimately, you must accept yourself. You must agree what kind of person, artist, voice, you perceive is within you and go along with that in all you do. After a point, there is no time to make yourself over if it is even possible and, imposter or not, you find you must be who you believe you are.

Vision: I stepped out the door to answer nature's call after a full morning and early afternoon of numbers filling my head—computerizing this year's calf crop—noticed the Brahman herd, across the yard in the pasture nearby. Cows black and white we'd put with a Brahman bull several months back, now in the fresh pasture (as we'd moved them only this morning). Nowadays it's hard to tell what has and hasn't been grazed, all so short, but they know, all heads down, young, old, grazing, scarfing it up without a second to waste, these waning hours of day, darkness (May Darkness Restore) a moment away, and they're still at it—like mosquitos on my arm gathering a blood meal, everything biting the earth for all its worth. Unspoken prayer. Eucharist.

Visit to Miami to cousin Valrae's, we took a trip to Fairchild Gardens to wind up at the Butterfly House. Valrae insisted we go. We crossed three thresholds to get in (perfection never easily accessible, they check what goes in and what comes out). It's a theoretical space—pure—a repository of innocence. How this comes to you full in the face at first sight, these windless, breathless creatures, ten thousand filling the air like falling, drifting petals of flowers animated upon some course that only seems like aimlessness. Time spent observing this only confuses things further. Squadrons of "like" flit by. There are mock chases that dissolve into irresolution, all prism-like: tiny pieces shimmering in the air. And there is hunger, procreation, determination taking place discreetly but in ceaseless motion. I sat awhile to soak it all in and fell into a reverie, realizing it would be a small matter to stay here forever save for other pressing circumstances. I have no doubt one could, given time, be healed of the world in this space. Would any of us settle for that? This is the only place I know a pure test could be conducted.

In a butterfly house there is nothing to despise.

Life is work—work is life.

Did Heaven first put it all inside a fence built upon certain hope, thinking things might work that way, like the Butterfly House at Fairchild. The plan soon fell apart, as it was most likely to do. Now we are gone. We are the fence.

Another Letter to Rick Campbell

As you read on your Zoom last evening . . . I watched from my iPhone,
the vagrant signal would come and go, but your words shone through,
remaining strong and (may I confess?) I was standing in a swimming
pool all the while up to my chest—the device propped upon the deck
coping against a glass of whiskey. It's almost difficult to believe how
the twenty-first century offers such juxtaposition. Across the way, the
western sky was taking place, sun already set, and a large formation
of clouds climbing into heaven as still-illumined veils of rain fell
between its layers so far away they almost seemed something else.

As I realized from the tiny screen it was brighter out on Alligator Point,
where you sat reading, face not quite in silhouette, than my dusking,
wet, protracted omniscience at the edge of a pasture, 250 miles down
peninsula on the other coast. I sensed darkness descending upon the
earth like a soft veil, south to north, and we, soon to follow, giving ourselves over to that certain peace continued in our dreams when the time
comes to close our eyes.

As you read in your measured, wistful manner, mixing each poem from
your traipse through life out of precedent, and often disparate stories, I
imagined you always aimed at and heading toward certain nothingness
and was left wondering for myself and my own life if we all might be
writing toward our ultimate dissolution from the world. You said as much
in the end, just as my signal began to fail, for I'd started the program
unwittingly without enough power and had to suffer your small dying
coupled with day's end and, last of all, the inescapable arrival of the dark.

Old Cow Museum

Like soldiers from the front, they come hobbling—
veterans of time's war—dragging limbs, comporting
brokenness—shambling on to assemble at the trough.
The heifer with a turned back foot is always in the lead,
maimed in calf-hood in a bovine crush, and culled
from the August load to stow here unsalable, where
she's grown, got bred out of season when a Brahma
bull spirited in and fertilized her like Danae.

The elderly blind dam smells her way to feed—outpaced
by the throng. We can't send her to market—the maze
opened on the trailer door as grim as her own *labyrinth*
—where and how would she go? They'd foot us a bill
for the pathetic parody played out. Here she stays until
death closes her paddock of memory: every shallow and rise
branch, and barb to learn again in her daily trace unless
she must follow her ear—or reckon the air.

Time stands still in the Old Cow Museum, *time present, time
past,* empties and fills the wombs of calf streams. Time of no
season, no accounting as the daily orb arrives to no consequence.
Where the crippled brahma that can't make it down the lane, glows
in the distance like a cumulonimbus over the Bahamas. She
calved, her first year in captivity, whelp—slight as her udder—
melted into the woodwork soon as we caught sight of him.
Here she stays, barren augury

of an unwhispered beatitude—violating every scruple of
cattle-breeding—companion to the arthritic angus matron
bought one year in the Carolinas at the end of a sale. *Attrition*
could be her name as she struggles to her portion like your
grandmother through the aisles of the grocer, cries loudest
when Sunday's brunch must wait til after church.
And every calving season orphans emerge—

to count among the *world's brood,* be added in:
the first timer's *get* she wouldn't own, an unclaimed twin,
daughter of the cancer-eye cow that withered away two
months shy of the wean, a listless starveling of the fretful
Madonna of the swollen teats—taken and given to shoulders
and wits, and wastrel whose mammy up and died mid-winter,
she—wild as a snake—to be gotten out and finessed
into this house of mishap; anyone in this business

needs what they contain: an out-of-the-way place,
the quelling grains, and peace of ancient dames.
At the end of suffering there is a door.
And some bright morning, we'll find another gone
off to the unfenced field, a shadow curled beneath
a bough; the collect of leather and bone, gather of
manure; birds already there. And what we'd always taken
for the wind, an unceasing benediction.

Seven Rises

I

2/2/22 Wednesday

Morning resembles modern art, an unbroken line
of light, cast between twin deep blue planes hanging
upon a bright yellow canvas of sky stretching
toward heaven.

Now earthbound things brighten—change perceptibly.
Contours of cloud mimic the jagged, umber horizon
of trees in upwellings whose sources remain
a mystery.

They say the saw-toothed appearance of that line in
the ocean at the edge of the world on windblown days
implies a difficult sea and what is there, you must
believe. The orb arrives, and all art crashes to the ground.

II

2/3/22 Thursday

Three handfuls of pink powder cast upon a pale
sapphire sky.

We let the heifers come west late yesterday afternoon—
heard them crying and discovered a broken water line,
the empty trough. Now they scatter like black pepper
upon the land, grazing in low light as natterings of calves
go unanswered by their mammies.

I wipe my brow, the listless air a damp hand on my face.
Early this week came a Polar Express bearing down on us,
ringing the chimes outside our door, stealing our grass.
We're in a hard way, fields burned, hay on order—if any
to be found. *None til Tuesday*, Thea texts. This is Thursday.

The road is quiet across the way, no traffic. I don't care
to hear another sound the rest of the day.

III

2/4/22 Friday

Early light fills the heavens like a thin-skinned old-fashioned
lamp shade. Mist has slender façade as fuzzy-white underlines beneath sentences of trees written on the distance, and
if I should speak of everything, there is little sound, animal
or machine this morning such that one wonders what is there
about Friday, would make it so?

Quiet is welcome in this season of hunger after the week's first
days of bedlam and loss. The orb appears at last, smearing light
all over the sky like butter on bread suddenly enlivening local
fauna. Two squirrels in an altercation just chased one another
across the entire yard on limbs and fronds of six different
species of trees.

IV

2/5/22 Saturday

A lone calf's voice is crying where it's not supposed to be, then
goes quiet. Orange cracks of dawn begin opening the sky
yet it's still too dark to investigate vagaries of sound.

Two dim bodies of cloud hang in the east: one, a gigantic breaking
wave, lifting out of the sea of grass and trees, the other seemingly
drawn from the sky where it remains.

There is no movement, only lightening and a startling of haze
from the earth's resume of silence. This spoken, there's suggestion
of much more to come.

Later, a softening into familiarity of the world rendering
visible. Now I can see the calf, his voice mollified by risen
light, and all matters coming to fruition.

By what magic does mist suddenly rise and claim the whole
land, dissolving like a misremembered prayer?

V

2/6/22 Sunday

The fifth rise will be different. We've come to a new place in the dark;
breath of the world in movement, chimes—hanging just outside the door,
in the trees—now answering. Coolness arrives, invades my writing
space, surrounds where I sit in jacket and pajamas. Soft whisperings
in the trees accompany lovely low singing, seeming at times to sound
on its own, then dies into the air.

Did I neglect to say things to my father when he was alive?

A poem I read last night made me wonder. Like the poet, I trusted
the silence kept between us, same as drove my mother away.
I shouldn't have blamed her for leaving.

Now there's a train, a low rumble, farther than it seems—two hours
before daylight—the horn like something crying—town by town,
carrying its sadness.

Emptiness and silence between men. Are they like mornings of stillness
in the air—no whisper or chime—world changed enough already.

VI

2/7/22 Monday

Fog. As if we don't live anywhere. East is west and the obverse.
Did the world rise into the clouds as we slept, and decide to stay?
Yesterday the sun never came up, but hid behind a shroud, pulled
over the face of the sky. Today, the world beyond has disappeared
and perhaps all my concerns with it.

The chime sways almost soundlessly, touching a single, almost in-
audible note. There is dripping as if morning's advent could reverse.
Everything need only descend, like this thick sky over a land dressed
in its bed clothes. Perhaps, we'll soon have our day, a new season,
and whatever next comes to hand.

Rise? You might ask. I shall wait instead for everything to fall.

VII

2/8/22 Tuesday

The world's breath, this morning: lifts and scatters leaves of paper
on the table and floor—deciduous, human matter—fallen. Clatter
of town, road, and equipment is in the air. To the west: cattle crying,
mine traffic, and the pump across the yard—switching on and off—
exhaling drafts of water to troughs in the fields when pressure drops.

I'm the stenographer of sound this gray morning, kept at my desk by slow-
risen light. Frond, leaf, petal, and branch, all astir, but the chime curiously
silent. The east herd gathers into a dark mass as if caught and held
against strands, two fence-lines away. And a sky slowly lifts but there
is no rift, no entry place for the orb—only a solemn scrim stretching over
and covering the brown drab emptiness.

Every day is a new puzzle to solve: open or shut gates on far fields
of the ranch that took the hardest wind and cold. Cattle move to the next
pasture when we let them in, walking without stopping—no heads down—
so one wonders where they are going. All day the orb remains hidden.
When they were determining the months, they took days away from this one
out of sheer dread.

Winter's Edge

Poetry escapes me of late, not that it's gone.
Across the way, a white cow brightens the blonde
winter pasture before a stand of palms cast in shadow.

I felt old last night when we didn't go out—my wife
said to me as we sat with coffee in the quiet morning.
—*It made me unhappy.*

Now she's in the kitchen in lively phone-chatter to a friend.
I remain, glimmering field empty.

A lizard climbs the screen.

Coda

Don't think your little sips
of life aren't using up
these Monday–Sunday leaps
upon the weeks.

Time flows ever by
like water through a tile
killing you anew
every little while.

List of Images

Notes

"Semen Testing the Herd Bulls," pg. 4

Everything that matters in life flows through tubes.

Georg Lichtenberg was a German physicist, which in some way might explain this otherwise eccentric and humorous epigraph. His private notebooks or scrapbooks exerted a strong influence on subsequent German philosophy, including the writings of Freud, Nietzsche, and Wittgenstein.

I see a whole semi-load of calves! is a chute-side quote of Dr. Kerry McGeehee, veteran of the Okeechobee Dairy Vet Corps upon spying a just-collected semen sample.

"Verities," pg. 9

The epigraph comes from conversation with Wendell one Sunday as we were looking up the hillside in the bright summer morning and talking about the recent restoration of his barn he could only justify by keeping certain loveliness intact.

"English isn't," pg. 17

References Stephen Dobyns's poem "The Gardener" from *Velocities: New and Selected Poems 1966-1992.*

"Pine Heart," pg. 26

In her *Diary from Dixie*, Mary Chestnut declared, "Thank God for pine knots," during the siege of Richmond in the American Civil War. It is easy to imagine, when fuel grew scarce, such sylvan remnants available to be found and gathered by denizens in the rural outskirts of the city.

"Canoe Creek Road," pg. 40

The poem originated from a trip of several years ago at the end
of a difficult spring drought on a drive to a Florida Beef Council
meeting at the Florida Cattlemen's Association Headquarters. The
road is a "back way" to Kissimmee, connecting Hwy 441 to SR
192, passing through, as described, much Florida native range and
"cattle country." I was able to employ a voice/text memo feature
on my iPhone to record much of the poem as I drove, overcome
by the urge to write as I made my way through the alluring
conditions of the landscape, and returned on the same route after
the meeting, to clarify my impressions.

"Cleaning Out from beneath the Scales," pg. 46

Each year, every device in the state of Florida upon which weight or
volume is measured and sold must be tested and approved by the
FL Dept. of Agriculture, and consumer services and cattle scales are
no exception. Technicians arrive unannounced with 5,000 pounds
of weights off-loaded with extendable booms and hauled in to
check the accuracy of the scales, required to be accurate within a
narrow parameter. Feeder calves are the annual produce of most
Florida beef cattle operations. Within a hundred-mile radius of Lake
Okeechobee is the largest concentration of 500-head lots of calves
in the US, and around the time of the summer solstice, western
order-buyers come to line up as many loads as they can for back-
grounding and feedlot operations mostly in the west and midwest.

"Soul Lost," pg. 52

Gary Stewart was born May 28, 1944 in Jenkins, Kentucky and
died December 16, 2003, fifteen miles south of my hometown
in Fort Pierce. He was an American country music musician and
songwriter known for his distinctive vibrato voice and a repertoire
influenced by southern rock. In the peak of his popularity, *Time*
magazine described him as the "King of Honkytonk." He often
returned from Nashville to play bars and haunts with friends of
local acquaintance, sometimes inviting them to return with him to
the main stages of country music.

"Folly," pg. 53

Image accompanying the news story of the "Great Elephant Ear Challenge," as covered in the May 6, 1932 *Palm Beach Post.*

"Poem of Edgar," pg. 62

In memoriam: George "Lucky" Edgar Straeffer, March 15, 1941–September 27, 2019

"Dirge," pg. 63

In memoriam: Katherine Grantley Sexton McCall, September 8, 1953–May 11, 2019

"RFK/RIP," pg. 66

Sixteen years ago, I dropped my wife and mother-in-law at the Kravits Center in West Palm Beach on a Sunday afternoon to attend the opera *Carmen* and went to the Norton Museum of Art to spend the next three hours revisiting their fabulous collection. In one of the galleries, I came upon an exhibition of photographs taken by *Look Magazine* staff photographer Paul Fusco from windows of the cars of Senator Robert Kennedy's funeral train on June 8, 1968, three days after he was shot at the Ambassador Hotel in Los Angeles. He'd won the California Presidential Primary and was giving his acceptance speech.

The photographs were novel in that Fusco trained his camera on many of the up to two million people along the 225-mile journey standing trackside where they seemed to appear from all walks of life, perhaps motivated by sadness and grief, curiosity, and the desire to pay their last respects. Words in quotation *(italicized)* came from essays by Norman Mailer, Evan Thomas, and Senator Edward Kennedy's eulogy delivered at his brother's service. Other quotes derived from Arthur Schlesinger and Kenny O'Donnell, all included in the book *RFK Funeral Train,* published in 2000 by Magnum Photos Inc., featuring a selection of the photographs. More quotations arose from testimonials recorded on video footage from televised coverage, featured in news programs on the anniversary of the train's passage.

The photography exhibition was so captivating that afternoon it was difficult for me to leave the gallery as I felt I'd walked into a time capsule. So many memories came flooding back to me from childhood. I went to the museum cafe for coffee and began drafting this poem which I finished, strangely enough, in early June of 2020, on almost the 52nd anniversary of the cortege. Paul Fusco since passed away July 15, 2020.

"World without Odis," pg. 71

Odis T. Bellamy Sr. was born in Orange Lake, Florida August 20, 1913, and served in the South Pacific as a machine gunner in the rank of Private First Class. He was a carpenter and maintenance man for Waldo Sexton and his family most of his life. He died March 27, 1997, and is buried in Gifford Cemetery. Only after I'd written the poem and spent half a lifetime with the wrong impression did I discover Odis had been stationed a short time in Wendover, UT Airforce Base, site of training for the 509th Composite Group which carried out the bombings of Hiroshima and Nagasaki. When he related to me he'd seen the *Tombic Bomb*, I now believe he meant he saw it in situ in the colossal Enola Gay B-29 hangar during his duty, prior to deployment of the fateful mission.

"In Yonder Fields," pg. 77

This poem is an adaptation from "In Flanders Fields," a WWI poem written in rondeau form by Canadian physician, Lieutenant Colonel John McCrae. It was written May 3, 1915, after McCrae presided over the funeral of a friend and fellow soldier, Lt. Alexis Helmer, who died in the second battle of Ypres. According to legend, fellow soldiers retrieved the poem after McCrae, initially dissatisfied, discarded it. It has become one of the most quoted poems of the war. The setting of "In Yonder Fields" takes in points of arrival and departure in beginning and aftermath for the myriad numbers of feeder calves of Florida's cow/calf industry sold to western stocker and feedlot operations around the summer solstice each year.

"The Mast," pg. 86

From Middle English/Old High German, "mast" refers to nuts, such as acorns, accumulated on the forest floors in early autumn, often serving as food for animals.

The ending phrase is taken from Ecclesiastes 3:1.

"Pictures of the Early Gods of Our Adolescence," pg. 93

The ending passage comes from Paul's first letter to the Corinthians.

"Sonnet on a Glass Snake," pg. 99

Glass lizard, also in the vernacular *glass* or *joint snake,* is the object of southern myth and folklore. In the genus *Ophisaurus,* these legless lizards have shiny, scaled bodies and, unlike snakes, have eyelids and ear openings. They are native to south and central US and to Eurasia.

"Ars Poetica, Obstetrics, Painting, and the Rough Draft," pg.102

Ars Poetica, or the "Art of Poetry," is a poem first written around 19 BC by Horace, the leading Roman lyric poet during the time of the emperor Augustus, by which he advised poets on the art of writing poetry and drama. It has become a form in itself and inspired poets over millennia ever since it was written.

"Our Rivers Are Hiding," pg. 104

Refers in part to the two rivers originating in Indian River County, setting of many of these poems. Both the St. Sebastian and the St. Johns rivers flow north and comprise areas of reclamation; the former, a subject of this poem. The Sebastian River Water Control Chapter 298 District was created by Florida's legislature in 1927, and the St. John's River Water Management District is a regional governing body covering much of east coastal Florida from our county to Jacksonville, FL, where it meets the Atlantic Ocean along the seaboard. Our family's Treasure Hammock Ranch makes up part of the headwaters of the St. Sebastian River.

"A Suite in Minutes," pg. 106

Is written in Minute form as introduced by Cathy Smith Bowers in her book *The Abiding Image*, in which she describes: "a poem consisting of sixty syllables with a syllabic line count of 8,4,4,4—8,4,4,4—8,4,4,4. The form also consists of rhyming couplets that often seem an elegant weaving of Elizabethan sonnet and early-Eastern haiku." The creator of the form was Verna Lee Hinegardner, a past poet laureate of Arkansas, whose official definition of the form included strict iambic meter, capitalization and punctuation like prose, and capturing *slices of life*. The form also appears in the poems "Prodigal" and "Empty Nest" in other sections of this volume.

The subject of David in Florida derives from a copy of the famous sculpture carved by Michelangelo Buonarotti in 1501 when he was twenty-six years old. The replica is only one of two exact copies of the seventeen-foot, ten-ton creation rendered by Sollazzini and Sons' Studio of Florence, Italy, out of a solid piece of Pietrasanta Carrara marble from the same quarry, Fantiscritti in Miseglia, Tuscany, as Michelangelo's masterpiece.

Made in 1963 for the New York World's Fair, it was moved to Buena Park, California in 1965 where it stood for forty-two years and was then acquired by *Ripley's Believe It or Not!*, and in May of 2007, was erected inside a small, hedge-lined recess out front of the renowned *Ripley's* tourist attraction in St. Augustine, FL.

"Bright Future," pg. 110

Is an ekphrastic poem written from the photograph "Men Loading Watermelons onto Wagons at Wilser's Stock Farm, Tampa, FL, ca. 1922," in Burgert Brothers Photographic Collection for an anthology project of Yellow Jacket Press commemorating early days of Tampa, Florida.

"Portals," pg. 113

Many excerpts and anecdotes of "Portals" come from pages of journals kept since 1973, comprising a body of writing beginning as a class project during my first year of college as assigned by a beloved English professor, Cathy Turner, and continuing to this day. The journal, now over 125 volumes, continues to grow and is written and drawn from my life working on Treasure Hammock Ranch.

"Old Cow Museum," pg. 122

At the end of suffering there is a door, page 123, line 18, is taken from Louise Glück's poem, "The Wild Iris."

"Little Sips," pg. 135

Features an image of an early fence brace still in service after more than eighty years, built by men long ago graved. The design has now been replaced by modern compression braces employing pressure-treated posts and diagonal cross wire.

Sean Sexton was born in Indian River County and grew up on his family's Treasure Hammock Ranch. He divides his time between managing a 700-acre cow-calf and seed stock operation, painting, and writing. He has kept daily sketch and writing journals since 1973. He is author of *Blood Writing*, Anhinga Press, 2009, *The Empty Tomb*, University of Alabama Slash Pine Press, 2014, *Descent*, Yellow Jacket Press, 2018, and *May Darkness Restore*, Press 53, 2019. He has performed at the National Cowboy Poetry Gathering in Elko, NV, Miami Book Fair International, Other Words Literary Conference in Tampa, FL and the High Road Poetry and Short Fiction Festival, in Winston-Salem, NC. He has garnered several nominations for Pushcart Prizes, and received a Florida Individual Artist's Fellowship in 2001.

He is a board member of the Laura Riding Jackson Foundation (Lauraridingjackson.org) and founding event chair of the Annual Poetry and Barbeque held each April, now in its tenth year. He also co-founded Poetry and Organ Advent and Lenten Concert Series at Community Church in Vero Beach, FL (ccovb.org) featuring nine concerts annually, attracting poets from all over the US. He became inaugural Poet Laureate of Indian River County in 2016.

CPSIA information can be obtained
at www.ICGtesting.com
Printed in the USA
BVHW040342060323
659681BV00001B/14